AI and Authorship in Scholarly Communication

AI and Authorship in Scholarly Communication explores the role of artificial intelligence (AI) as it pertains to scholarly research and writing.

Explaining what AI is and how it can be used by scholars, the book also focuses on aspects with the potential to change the scholarly communication landscape. Bringing together research on AI and writing from the scholarly literature in LIS and beyond, the book weaves together information about essential topics relating to AI and authorship. In laying out the primary concerns surrounding AI in the field of scholarly communication, Moulaison-Sandy considers how those concerns map to norms and practices in research and writing. The book likewise explores the future landscape of scholarly communication, an environment in which AI will continue to play an important role.

AI and Authorship in Scholarly Communication will be of great interest to scholars, students, and practitioners and will be particularly useful to those studying AI or authorship from a library and information science (LIS) perspective. Researchers or practitioners working in higher education or with learning technologies will also find much to interest them within the pages of the book.

Heather Moulaison-Sandy, PhD, is Associate Professor at the iSchool at the University of Missouri, where she also holds a joint appointment with the French Department. Moulaison-Sandy studies and teaches in areas relating to scholarly communication, metadata, and AI.

AI and Authorship in Scholarly Communication

Writing with Intelligence

Heather Moulaison-Sandy

Routledge
Taylor & Francis Group
LONDON AND NEW YORK

First published 2025
by Routledge
4 Park Square, Milton Park, Abingdon, Oxon OX14 4RN

and by Routledge
605 Third Avenue, New York, NY 10158

Routledge is an imprint of the Taylor & Francis Group, an informa business

British Library Cataloguing-in-Publication Data
A catalogue record for this book is available from the British Library

ISBN: 978-1-032-94358-9 (hbk)
ISBN: 978-1-032-94361-9 (pbk)
ISBN: 978-1-003-57032-5 (ebk)

DOI: 10.4324/9781003570325

Typeset in Times New Roman
by Apex CoVantage, LLC

Contents

Acknowledgments

This book was supported in part through funding by the University of Missouri's Great Books Program. I am grateful, as well, to Lena Marvin for feedback on an early draft of the manuscript.

1 Introduction

Artificial intelligence (AI) has emerged as a disruptive technology on par with the advent of the printing press or the internet;[1] the excitement that AI has garnered since the public launch of ChatGPT in November 2022 has been difficult to contain. AI is unquestionably affecting society as a whole, with AI-powered systems increasingly finding their way into daily life.

AI invites polemics, with cautionary tales emerging alongside tracts that convey unbridled enthusiasm. Leaving aside the much broader context in which society will have to negotiate the contributions and limitations of AI going forward, this book instead focuses on the very narrow field of scholarly communication – specifically, the work done by scholars, who do research and then write up and share their work, as well as the associated practices and actions of scholarly publishers formally publishing the work.

As scholarly communication adapts in light of the appearance of increasingly ubiquitous AI-powered systems, so too will the scholarly record be transformed.

As generations of scholars become increasingly used to AI-powered tools, expecting their use and taking them for granted, these tools will become as common and integrated as spell-check and grammar check; indeed, predictive text is already commonly suggested through word processing software, and documents are inviting users to "chat" with them using AI. Intelligence, the artificial kind, is supporting scholars in their work, especially in the write-up. It is fair to say that writing with intelligence is here; what remains to be seen is how that, and other uses of AI, might affect these and other practices that shape the scholarly record.

The interest in AI that has accompanied the release of ChatGPT has also led to questions about the future of scholarly communication and the potential for far-reaching impacts on the scholarly record, especially as the weaknesses of large language models (LLMs) like ChatGPT have begun to reveal themselves.

DOI: 10.4324/9781003570325-1

Writing With Intelligence

Scholars wish to write *intelligently*, that is to say, they wish to write *with intelligence*. In the era of ChatGPT, writing with *artificial* intelligence is easier than ever. At the same time, LLMs are not infallible, and their limitations for scholarship give pause. Their ease of use and apparent simplicity might make them enticing to use them alongside more traditional approaches to research, writing, and publishing, but scholars engaging with AI will need to keep in mind that writing with intelligence requires the oversight of human actors. AI output can never be accepted without close inspection and a critical (human) eye. In other words, AI can be an important tool in a scholar's repertoire, but the scholar's intelligence is the one on which work will ultimately be based.

This book explores the relationships between human actors, the environment in which scholarly communication is carried out, and the affordances and constraints that AI represents in this setting. The related notions of authorship and scholarly communication, and in particular ways that scholars work *with* intelligence are explored: human intelligence is (at least for now) what guides scholarship, but *artificial* intelligence represents an important way that scholarly communication and the authorship practices that contribute to a robust scholarly record are adapting to the current scholarly environment.

Scholarly Communication and the Scholarly Record

Scholarly communication is a complex system in which a number of actors engage. This short book focuses on the mechanisms scholars use to communicate with each other, generally in a way that is formal, and especially in ways that are managed and overseen by scholarly publishers. The permanent scholarly record and the way that it supports the current and future creation of new knowledge will be impacted by AI, and this book considers how that pertains most readily to formal scholarly communication-based activities such as authorship.

Synthesizing a number of sources, Christine L. Borgman describes scholarly communication as "the study of how scholars in any field (e.g., physical, biological, social, and behavioral sciences, humanities, technology) use and disseminate information through formal and informal channels."[2] More recently, Rick Anderson states that "the term [scholarly communication] refers to the many different ways in which authors and creators of scholarly and scientific work share information with each other and with the rest of the world about the work they are doing."[3] Because of the breadth of the definition of scholarly communication, informal methods of communication including social media and even email can also be considered. The primary emphasis considered in this book, however, is on the processes that lead to the establishment of the scholarly record, or to the formal record of scholarly activity that supports the work of scholars as they make advancements in their field.

The scholarly record captures formal, scholarly works that have been published. For the scholarly record to be meaningful, it must be trustworthy. Trust is one of the end goals, generated through the creation of scholarly products as free as possible from all varieties of biases and flaws. In other words, the scholarly record reflects a series of criteria that denote high-quality scholarship. M. V. Dougherty considers books and journal articles from well-established sources as the primary contribution to the scholarly record, and describes six hallmarks of these items: 1) they complement and extend knowledge; 2) they have clear authorship/attribution; 3) they are formally published by an academic publisher; 4) they are retained in academic libraries and in relevant databases, and as such, 5) they serve as the foundation for future entries into the scholarly record; and finally 6) they belong to a particular discipline.[4]

Meeting Conditions for Inclusion in the Scholarly Record

Of the six conditions for inclusion in the scholarly record mentioned earlier, three conditions emerge as being particularly relevant to this book and the question of the use of AI in scholarly communication. The *knowledge condition*, the *authorship condition*, and the *discipline condition* relate to the work scholars carry out as well as the roles that AI can play in the process. As scholars engage in their craft and write up their work for consumption by their peers, addressing these conditions is paramount, as they allow scholars to earn trust, take responsibility for their work while reaping the benefits, and situate themselves and their work in the larger body of work in their field.

"The Knowledge Condition"

The first condition for inclusion in the scholarly record, as identified by Dougherty, is that an item meet the *knowledge condition*; it must make "a putative contribution to a discipline's collective body of truth claims."[5] Authors must produce content that is new and in alignment with expectations for the field. For example, empirical research, theory building, and systematic reviews all might contribute to a scholar's field in different ways, and all are new creations that provide novel insights to move the field forward. Fundamentally, therefore, creativity and productivity on the part of an academic author and researcher can be seen to go hand in hand.[6]

Creativity is not something that happens on a whim in works that find their way into the scholarly record. Among other things, creativity in scholarship comes from the culmination of a scholar's training: authors must have an understanding of the field, intuition in identifying and solving problems, the knowledge and ability to apply the kind of rigor and structure to successfully investigate the questions, the wisdom to interpret and communicate the results, and access to the infrastructure in which to carry out and write up the work.

Intuition in regard to what one knows can be credited as one way that these problems can be identified and subsequently addressed.[7] For this, no one would expect someone uninitiated in the field of military history to develop a cutting-edge approach to analyzing the military tactics employed during the 209 BCE Dazexiang uprising in China against the Qin dynasty. After mastery in an area is reached, a burst of activity, which manifests itself as productivity, follows.[8] Presumably, good intuition leads to identifying good research questions and appropriate research methodologies, which ultimately leads to novel results that move the discipline forward. Within the intellectual confines of a field and its approaches and literature, scientists must innovate. By creating and sharing new knowledge, disciplines move themselves forward. That work, however, must be trustworthy, and it must show evidence of the highest level of academic integrity.

Academic Integrity

In producing their work for others in their immediate area, scholars adhere to a set of values in the hopes of addressing the conundrum Wiebe E. Bijker and colleagues identify when they ask: "How can we understand the authority of science while recognizing its socially constructed nature?"[9] Humans helm science, at least for now. Facts must still be interpreted in light of principles and theories. Differing approaches to interpretation can lead science to be mistrusted by the public at large. One way to earn trust and affirm public accountability is through adherence to ethical standards that support academic integrity. Adherence to ethical standards also garners public support.[10]

The fundamental values of academic integrity have been defined as honesty, trust, fairness, respect, responsibility, and courage;[11] these dovetail nicely with the values of research integrity as defined by the US Office of Research Integrity (ORI): honesty, accuracy, efficiency, and objectivity.[12] All of these must be reflected in work that is part of the scholarly record, and these values guide the ethical behavior required for authorship in scientific writing.

Conversely, academic misconduct is presented as a serious violation of these norms that could lead students to fail a class or be expelled from the institution or that could strip more seasoned researchers of their posts (e.g., Diederik Stapel)[13]. Despite the serious consequences, large numbers of both undergraduate and graduate students nonetheless admit to academic dishonesty[14] and junior researchers also admit to a host of *bad behaviors* that run counter to principles of academic integrity.[15] Not all researchers act ethically under the best of circumstances, eroding trust and opening the system to criticism and suspicion, with the potential for ruining the good reputation not only of themselves and their institutions but also their publishers, their disciplines, and scientific inquiry overall.

"The Authorship Condition"

Another relevant condition for inclusion to the scholarly record identified by Dougherty is the *authorship condition*, wherein authors take responsibility for the work that is produced. In taking responsibility for that work, scholars claim ownership over the intellectual content. Responsibility must be asserted, ensuring the trustworthiness of the work, including its academic integrity. One benefit of ownership is access to priority claims in terms of intellectual content. Priority claims can beget prestige and notoriety, statuses that are often highly sought by researchers.

Ownership and Responsibility

Although publishers do their best to warrant that the scholarly record is comprised of trustworthy works, ultimately authors are responsible for their creations. Authors own their intellectual content. They participate in the "dangers of writing," potentially leaving them legally accountable for the work they own, but are "conferred the benefits of property,"[16] including the benefits the academy and the disciplines bestow on authors. In other words, before benefits can be reaped, responsibility must be taken.

Responsibilities of that owned text include ensuring the highest standards in the work that bears one's name, along with the enactment of ethical approaches to research and writing. Conceptualizing research, carrying it out, writing it up, and seeing it published all take a substantial amount of effort. Solo-authored works are increasingly rare; accordingly, in a shared authorship environment, all authors should be responsible for the content they have published. And by the same token, all who have authored the piece should be included in the byline to enable them to benefit from the work.[17]

Priority Claims and Notoriety

Successful authors enjoy one of the benefits of authorship: recognition for originating the ideas.[18] Establishing priority claims is an important and historically necessary part of scientific authorship; it settles "priority conflicts" and formalizes the scholarly record in the process.[19] Although approaches have changed over time,[20] the printed word as part of the scholarly record is the most reliable way to establish priority. Authorship of scientific writing is nonetheless an excellent way to earn notoriety that leads to prestige, which is a commodity that is highly valued in academia. Notoriety is a positive thing given "one of the objectives in this milieu [i.e., academia] is to 'make a name for oneself.'"[21] For the scholarly endeavor, the payment in prestige and the ability to assert priority represent an immense professional value to the author. For scholars who are under pressure to publish or perish, priority claims and notoriety might be less important than the simple fact of having secured enough publications to remain employed.

Researchers interested in practices in scholarly communication have observed that abundances in notoriety beget additional abundances in notoriety. Robert K. Merton, sociologist of science, describes what he terms the *Matthew effect* in 1968.[22] Based on work of his student, Harriet Zuckerman, in interviewing Nobel laureates in the US, Merton observes that those who have notoriety seem to accumulate additional notoriety almost effortlessly. Named for the biblical scenario involving Saint Matthew where the rich get richer and the poor get poorer, the Matthew effect has been applied in a number of scholarly environments, where those who have more notoriety are observed to attain more.[23] More notoriety allows one privileges, perhaps to access better resources, more infrastructure, and higher-quality support, enhancing the potential for even more priority claims.

"The Discipline Condition"

Dougherty likewise describes the *discipline condition*, where works in the scholarly record must belong to a specific field of study; among other things, this allows for the items to be correctly and accurately assessed and placed in an academic publication. Works demonstrate their affiliations with a specific discipline, or demonstrate their interdisciplinarity, in part through the sources they cite and the methods they adopt.

Citing and Crediting Appropriate Sources

If "[t]he institutional goal of science is the extension of certified knowledge,"[24] then tracing the flow of ideas is an essential part of authorship in scholarly communication. Authors are understood to have a necessary intellectual relationship with their antecedents and are also expected to internalize what they learn and produce something new.[25] In this context, the attribution of ideas or otherwise "standing on the shoulders of giants" by drawing from established sources is a necessary part of what scholars do.

Among other things, for novelty to be apparent, research must start from a point of departure in a given field; this will be evident in the works that are cited as a foundation for the research. By clearly identifying sources and crediting them, the tracing and tracking of ideas can take place. This enables the clear tracing of ownership and responsibility, reinforcing trustworthiness through the use of appropriate, vetted sources that adhere to strictures of academic integrity. In the process, priority claims are shored up and the notoriety of those who preceded is reinforced.

Adopting Appropriate Approaches

By exhibiting knowledge of the relevant extant literature and by employing appropriate methodologies, authors adhere to the approaches adopted by their disciplines. In some disciplines, empirical research will be most appropriate, with qualitative approaches being standard in certain situations. In others, quantitative research methods might be the norm. In yet others, theory building might be the most appropriate way to address the questions that are asked. In other words, the *methodology* can differ vastly in scholarship, from adopting a Hegelian dialectic to explicating a passage in a novel, to carrying out empirical, data-driven analyses of temperature fluctuations in a laboratory environment or sequencing a gene – the requirement for it to be science is that it be systematic and recognized by the field's researchers, and approaches can very rightly mean many things to many researchers.

Ensuring Transparency and Reproducibility

Related to citing and crediting sources and to adopting approaches that are appropriate is the notion of transparency in the products of scholarly inquiry. Among other things, transparency in research provides a lens into the rigor with which the research was undertaken and is a key way of supporting trustworthiness. By opening the research and writing process for analysis and critique, transparent research promotes reproducibility or ability for external researchers to reproduce the results produced and conclusions drawn. Transparent research, from access to information about the methodology, data sources, and results, allows research to be evaluated and, in many cases, to be tested. The transparent references to sources that are the basis for the research is also an important step to providing transparent insight into its place in the extant body of knowledge on a topic.

Situating Artificial Intelligence (AI)

Artificial intelligence (AI) is not new. In fact, the term "artificial intelligence" is largely acknowledged to have been coined by John McCarthy in 1955 and to have been applied to concepts like computers playing chess against human opponents.[26] According to a publication from 2007 by McCarthy, AI "is the science and engineering of making intelligent machines, especially intelligent computer programs."[27] IBM describes AI as "a field, which combines computer science and robust datasets, to enable problem-solving."[28] The problems solved by AI can extend beyond games and scenarios with very specific, pre-defined rules. The artificial intelligence behind systems like ChatGPT, a large language model (LLM), produces content that is language-based in nature, though broadly speaking, generative AI systems can create a range of content such as text, images, and video based on the datasets used.[29]

When considering ideas that are new or otherwise challenging, metaphors are one way to help make concepts understandable. Metaphors are figures of speech that allow for a comparison between two things that are not similar.

The term "AI (artificial intelligence)" likens computer algorithms making predictions based on underlying data to human intelligence. Human intelligence is much more complex, however, than the ability to calculate based on previously encountered content. Although pointing out the flaws in a term might not help the term to be replaced, in this case, an analysis of a few of the high-level points can help the larger understanding of how scholarly communication may be impacted.

As AI and AI-powered systems have become increasingly prevalent and as concerns have emerged, metaphors have appeared in the literature. For example, systems like ChatGPT have been compared to stochastic parrots, where their uses of flawed and biased underlying data risk reinforcing hegemonic worldviews.[30] In addition, AI (especially systems like ChatGPT) has been put forth as being like a mirror that flatters its users, and that amplifies what it reflects rather than creating anything new.[31]

Specifically, when considering the writing task and the aspects that support *writing with intelligence,* two metaphors will be explored here in a bit of depth that will be revisited as the book progresses. These are the metaphor of an *anthropomorphized, human-like intelligence* (as opposed to a limited, "artificial" computer intelligence) and the metaphor of a *black box.*

Anthropomorphized Intelligence

Like computing in general, AI "is capable of performing tasks that conventionally require human intelligence, and even surpasses human capabilities in many challenging tasks that involve a large amount of data to analyze and learn from."[32] The aspect of computer's mimicking human intelligence was famously described by Alan Turing with a test that has come to be known as the Turing test, where a human is unable to discern a computer-based interlocutor from a human one. Turing first put forth this idea in 1950, and it has since permeated Western culture via systems such as ELIZA the chatbot, a system created in the 1960s. ELIZA could carry a conversation, though perhaps a bit strange at times; ELIZA did seem to pass the Turing test. ELIZA was, for example, an inspiration for HAL 9000 in the 1968 film *2001: A Space Odyssey*. Much of the current literature on the convincing nature of AI has emerged, however, in the past ten or so years.[33]

All told, the enthusiasm for the overall intelligence of AI systems seems to be borne out. AI is argued to be at parity with humans for several research-related and writing skills.[34] Systems like ChatGPT handily pass the Turing test, with some users believing they are sentient, attributing different aspects of human personalities to them (e.g., friendly or aloof). All of this helps these LLMs seem *intelligent*, in the same way that humans are. AI can be so convincingly human that even former Google employee Blake Lemoine, an engineer working in AI and who fundamentally should have known better, began to declare that AI systems were sentient and had feelings.[35] In other words, AI can fool even the brightest, most educated minds, even if

> AI does not include deeper human and animal abilities such as the creation of meaning, the connection with others and the ability to feel and think, except where aspects of meaning, connection, feeling and thinking can be encoded as data-in-data-out decision problems.[36]

As AI becomes increasingly common as a way to support decision-making, however, concerns have emerged. Warnings about "human-washing" machines by corporate and possibly military-related entities "while creating unrealistic perceptions of harmless, humanlike behavior" have been put forth as a way to attempt to mask more nefarious ends.[37] Concerns relating to how scholars and their publishers are relying on the limited yet dazzling prospects put forth by machine intelligence likewise have presented themselves, and these will be explored throughout the rest of the book, often in conjunction with the problem of the *black box* that AI represents.

Black Boxes

Today, systems that are AI-powered often involve the use of what are called *deep learning models*. IBM affirms,

> One potential weakness across them all is that deep learning models are often 'black boxes,' making it difficult to understand their inner workings and posing interpretability challenges. But this can be balanced against the overall benefits of high accuracy and scalability.[38]

In other words, AI algorithms and decision-making processes lack transparency, which is offset by the quality of their output. This lack of transparency has the potential to feed into the illusion of providing sentient insight into problems on the part of AI.

In general, technology that is not transparent is termed a *black box*, meaning the model presents a situation where the internal logic is obscured. Many AI systems are notoriously black boxes due to the way they are programmed. Black boxes are helpful because obscuring details of a process can allow users to focus on the results. However, as Changwu Huang and colleagues describe, the black box's lack of transparency and the inability of users and developers to understand what the algorithms are doing is a "downside of AI,"[39] and is one that creates deep ethical concerns in relation to the content that is produced. In fact, all three of the tenets of authorship in the realm of scholarly communication described here are flouted by the black box, and potentially some of the work done as part of the research process (depending on how the

AI is being applied to the problem) is also obscured. Another way of thinking of this is that the very aspects of AI that make it so appealing, especially when considering systems like ChatGPT or automated classification of data, are some of the biggest concerns when it comes to being able to use that content with confidence in scholarship.

In the case of systems like ChatGPT, convincing text from a convincingly anthropomorphized system is produced in response to simple prompts. However, that text does not come from a place of understanding. Most systems like ChatGPT do not clarify the sources of the ideas presented in the output, even if other systems, including Google's Gemini, purport to. For reasons of how the technology works, the sources behind the bits of text produced cannot generally be identified. Not only is intellectual property not respected, but its ownership cannot be clarified or endorsed. When there is no transparency, the adherence to the strictures of academic integrity and research integrity cannot be confirmed, and content is produced that is likely biased, inaccurate, lacking in integrity, or all three.

Questions can be raised as well about the algorithms themselves. Even if the underlying data is sound, the results are not necessarily free of problems. Even for bespoke AI systems, a black box element is likely still present. "In some extreme cases, systems become black boxes even to the researchers who created them."[40] Those that can share their code often do not. Out of the 40 "open source" AI text generator models analyzed by Andreas Liesenfeld and Mark Dingemanse in 2024, less than half provided open access to their code.[41]

Given the previous discussion about the importance of trust in scholarly communication and the exacting requirements for works that are part of the scholarly record, the black box aspect of AI can be problematic. All told, the black box aspect of AI is inconsistent with the tenets of scholarly communication – approaches that ultimately support a trustworthy scholarly record. They do this, among other things, by requiring on the part of authors the creativity, integrity, intellectual ownership and responsibility, attribution of sources, appropriate methodologies to address appropriate questions, and ultimately, transparency to support the scholarly record. The next chapter explores in greater depth the requirements of scholars when carrying out research and writing in this complex environment.

Notes

1 Mustafa Suleyman, *The Coming Wave: Technology, Power, and the Twenty-First Century's Greatest Dilemma*, 1st ed. (New York: Crown, 2023).
2 Christine L. Borgman, "Editor's Introduction," in *Scholarly Communication and Bibliometrics*, ed. Christine L. Borgman (Newbury Park: Sage Publications, 1990), 13.
3 Rick Anderson, *Scholarly Communication: What Everyone Needs to Know, What Everyone Needs to Know* (New York, NY: Oxford University Press, 2018), 5.

4 M. V. Dougherty, "Defining the Scholarly Record," in *Correcting the Scholarly Record for Research Integrity: In the Aftermath of Plagiarism*, ed. M. V. Dougherty (Cham: Springer International Publishing, 2018), 19–57, https://doi.org/10.1007/978-3-319-99435-2_2.

5 M. V. Dougherty, *Correcting the Scholarly Record for Research Integrity: In the Aftermath of Plagiarism, Research Ethics Forum*, vol. 6 (Cham: Springer International Publishing, 2018), 21, https://doi.org/10.1007/978-3-319-99435-2.

6 For example, Robert K. Merton, "The Normative Structure of Science, 1942," in *The Sociology of Science: Theoretical and Empirical Investigations* (Chicago: University of Chicago Press, 1973), 267–78, http://archive.org/details/robert_K_merton_the_sociology_of_science; Władysław Szafer, "Creativity in a Scientist's Life: An Attempt of Analysis from the Standpoint of the Science of Science," *Organon* 5 (1968): 3–39.

7 C.f., Michael Polanyi, *Personal Knowledge: Towards a Post-Critical Philosophy* (Chicago: University of Chicago Press, 1974); Szafer, "Creativity in a Scientist's Life."

8 Szafer, "Creativity in a Scientist's Life."

9 Wiebe E. Bijker, Roland Bal, and Ruud Hendriks, *The Paradox of Scientific Authority: The Role of Scientific Advice in Democracies* (The MIT Press, 2009), 2.

10 David B. Resnik et al., "Authorship Policies of Scientific Journals," *Journal of Medical Ethics* 42, no. 3 (March 2016): 199–202, https://doi.org/10.1136/medethics-2015-103171.

11 T. A. Fishman, ed., *The Fundamental Values of Academic Integrity*, 2nd ed. (International Center for Academic Integrity, 2014), https://www.academicintegrity.org/wp-content/uploads/2017/12/Fundamental-Values-2014.pdf.

12 Nicholas H. Steneck, *Introduction to the Responsible Conduct of Research* (ORI (Office of Research Integrity), August 2007), https://ori.hhs.gov/ori-introduction-responsible-conduct-research.

13 John M. Budd, "The Stapel Case: An Object Lesson in Research Integrity and Its Lapses," *Synesis: A Journal of Science, Technology, Ethics, and Policy* 4 (2013): G:47–G:53.

14 International Center for Academic Integrity, "Facts and Statistics," accessed October 14, 2024, https://academicintegrity.org/resources/facts-and-statistics.

15 Brian C. Martinson, Melissa S. Anderson, and Raymond de Vries, "Scientists Behaving Badly," *Nature* 435, no. 7043 (June 2005): 737–38, https://doi.org/10.1038/435737a.

16 Michel Foucault, "What Is an Author?," in *Language, Counter-Memory, Practice*, ed. Donald F. Bouchard, trans. Donald F. Bouchard and Sherry Simon (Ithaca, NY: Cornell University Press, 1977), 125.

17 Drummond Rennie and Annette Flanagin, "Authorship! Authorship!: Guests, Ghosts, Grafters, and the Two-Sided Coin," *Journal of the American Medical Association* 271, no. 6 (1994): 469–71.

18 Robert K. Merton, "Priorities in Scientific Discovery: A Chapter in the Sociology of Science," *American Sociological Review* 22, no. 6 (December 1957): 635, https://doi.org/10.2307/2089193.

19 Derek J. de Solla Price, *Little Science, Big Science – and Beyond* (New York: Columbia University Press, 1963), http://archive.org/details/littlesciencebig00pric.
20 Alex Csiszar, *Scientific Journal: Authorship and the Politics of Knowledge in the Nineteenth Century* (Chicago, IL: University of Chicago Press, 2020).
21 Pierre Bourdieu, *Homo Academicus* (Stanford University Press, 1988), 2.
22 Robert K. Merton, "The Matthew Effect in Science," *Science* 159, no. 3810 (1968): 56–63.
23 Daniel Rigney, *The Matthew Effect: How Advantage Begets Further Advantage* (New York: Columbia University Press, 2010).
24 Merton, "The Normative Structure of Science, 1942," 270.
25 Mary Carruthers, *The Book of Memory: A Study of Memory in Medieval Culture*, 2nd ed. (Cambridge, UK and New York: Cambridge University Press, 2008), 238.
26 Christopher Manning, *Artificial Intelligence Definitions* (Stanford University Human-Centered Artificial Intelligence, September 2020), https://hai.stanford.edu/sites/default/files/2020-09/AI-Definitions-HAI.pdf.
27 John McCarthy, "What Is Artificial Intelligence?," November 12, 2007, 2, http://www-formal.stanford.edu/jmc/, http://jmc.stanford.edu/articles/whatisai/whatisai.pdf.
28 IBM Research, "What Is Generative AI?," *IBM Research* (blog), April 20, 2023, para. 4, https://research.ibm.com/blog/what-is-generative-AI.
29 IBM Research, "What Is Generative AI?"
30 Muhammad Saad Uddin, "Stochastic Parrots: A Novel Look at Large Language Models and Their Limitations | Towards AI," April 13, 2023, https://towardsai.net/p/l/stochastic-parrots-a-novel-look-at-large-language-models-and-their-limitations.
31 Shannon Vallor, *The AI Mirror: How to Reclaim Our Humanity in the Age of Machine Thinking* (New York, NY: Oxford University Press, 2024).
32 Zhenghua Chen et al., "Survey on AI Sustainability: Emerging Trends on Learning Algorithms and Research Challenges [Review Article]," *IEEE Computational Intelligence Magazine* 18, no. 2 (May 2023): 60, https://doi.org/10.1109/MCI.2023.3245733.
33 David M. Berry, "The Limits of Computation: Joseph Weizenbaum and the ELIZA Chatbot," *Weizenbaum Journal of the Digital Society* 3, no. 3 (November 6, 2023), https://doi.org/10.34669/WI.WJDS/3.3.2.
34 For example, Tomer Simon, "The Scientist of the Scientist," *AI & Society* 39, no. 2 (April 2024): 803–4, https://doi.org/10.1007/s00146-022-01544-6.
35 Tiffany Wertheimer, "Blake Lemoine: Google Fires Engineer Who Said AI Tech Has Feelings," *BBC News*, July 22, 2022, https://www.bbc.com/news/technology-62275326.
36 Jennifer Chubb, Peter Cowling, and Darren Reed, "Speeding up to Keep up: Exploring the Use of AI in the Research Process," *AI & Society* 37, no. 4 (December 1, 2022): 1441, https://doi.org/10.1007/s00146-021-01259-0.
37 Gabriela Scorici, Mario D. Schultz, and Peter Seele, "Anthropomorphization and Beyond: Conceptualizing Humanwashing of AI-Enabled Machines," *AI & Society* 39, no. 2 (April 2024): 790, https://doi.org/10.1007/s00146-022-01492-1.

38 IBM, "What Is Deep Learning?," June 17, 2024, https://www.ibm.com/topics/deep-learning.
39 Changwu Huang et al., "An Overview of Artificial Intelligence Ethics," *IEEE Transactions on Artificial Intelligence* 4, no. 4 (August 2023): 802, https://doi.org/10.1109/TAI.2022.3194503.
40 Qin Zhu, "From Search and Discovery to Research and Reproducibility," *Online Searcher* 45, no. 6 (December 2021): 15.
41 Andreas Liesenfeld and Mark Dingemanse, "Rethinking Open Source Generative AI: Open Washing and the EU AI Act" (The 2024 ACM Conference on Fairness, Accountability, and Transparency, FAccT '24: The 2024 ACM Conference on Fairness, Accountability, and Transparency, Rio de Janeiro Brazil: ACM, 2024), 1774–87, https://doi.org/10.1145/3630106.3659005.

2 Engaging in Scholarly Writing

Engaging in scholarly writing is not for the faint of heart. It is also not for nonspecialists. Scientific, scholarly writing is different from reports, treatises, and other kinds of non-scholarly works. It is also, of course, different from the creative works of playwrights, novelists, and poets, and from the journalistic work of reporters. Scholarship is written for a specialized readership and is crafted based on expectations of the members of the field in which it is situated, garnering trust and moving the field forward. In other words, scholarly writing that becomes part of the scholarly record is how scholars write for other scholars in their field. An overview of the activities and practices of authorship are considered in this chapter, especially as they relate to the scholarly record and to the ways that AI can come to bear on the scholarly communication system.

The focus of this book is formal scholarly communication. Not all scholarly communication happens formally, though, and numerous informal ways of sharing research and writing exist. Specialized communication between scholars can take place largely unmediated in the public sphere, both in-person at conferences or via online platforms like X (formerly Twitter). Other opportunities for sharing ideas come through blogs or newsletters, and scholars can also post versions of unpublished work, including preprints, to preprint servers and institutional repositories. Yet the main way that scholars communicate officially with each other, especially over time, is through formal publications that are part of the scholarly record.

The scholarly record solidifies the final, formal version of a piece published through an academic outlet; this is the version of record and, among all possible versions, the most formal and the one that should be cited.[1] Historically, the formal means of communicating findings are also the ones that allow for the priority claims that are so valued by scholars and their employers and funders; therefore, the quintessential surrogate for researcher productivity is the list of publications, which is why that productivity, as represented through the scholarly record, will be the main focus here.

This chapter, therefore, considers in a basic way some of the salient elements of authorship in the scholarly communication ecosystem that can be affected by AI.

DOI: 10.4324/9781003570325-2

Criteria for Authorship

Scholars carry out research and write it up, and publishers generally oversee the rest, with continued input on the part of the author throughout the process. Like scholars, publishers are also subject to strict ethical standards to promote the trustworthiness of the final product. The Committee on Publication Ethics (COPE) is a group that supports the ethical work of editors and publishers, helping to ensure alignment between what authors need and what publishers do in support of the scholarly record.

Publishers, scholars, and style guides have presented a largely unified front in terms of who can be an author. To begin, authors must be human (not AI), and they must have responsibility for the text in a meaningful way (which AI cannot).

The International Committee of Medical Journal Editors (ICMJE) provides guidance into the kinds of human-driven contributions that scholarly publishers view as meriting authorship credit. Although these can be and often are critiqued as being too narrow, and are only intended to govern authorship contributions in medical journals which is the purview of the ICMJE, they offer a good point of departure for discussions of the kinds of activities that are needed to qualify for authorship status and inclusion in the byline of an article or as author of a book.

For the ICMJE, all four criteria must be satisfied, along with the identification tasks and confidence aspects mentioned subsequently:

1. Substantial contributions to the conception or design of the work; or the acquisition, analysis, or interpretation of data for the work; AND
2. Drafting the work or revising it critically for important intellectual content; AND
3. Final approval of the version to be published; AND
4. Agreement to be accountable for all aspects of the work in ensuring that questions related to the accuracy or integrity of any part of the work are appropriately investigated and resolved.
   In addition to being accountable for the parts of the work he or she has done, an author should be able to identify which co-authors are responsible for specific other parts of the work. In addition, authors should have confidence in the integrity of the contributions of their co-authors.[2]

All authors who meet these criteria should be included as authors, whereas contributors who only meet three of the criteria or who are not able to identify adequately who did what should not be included as authors and should instead be acknowledged in the acknowledgment section.[3] Rejecting an author who otherwise meets all four criteria because they do not know which of their coauthors wrote a particular section might seem a bit harsh, but the idea of accountability and a deep knowledge of the contributions is a big part of this equation – one that seems reasonable when there are two or three co-authors, but less feasible when there are hundreds, if not thousands.

Roles Associated With Scholarship

An expectation exists that not all work in scholarly communication is credited in the byline, and that additional roles exist that allow scholarship to come into existence and to take the form that it takes. As indicated by the ICMJE, even those whose work is fundamental to a project will not receive authorial credit if they are not familiar with the whole of the paper. These supporting roles, however, go far in enabling the functioning of the scholarly communication process and in supporting the creation of high-quality work to enter into the scholarly record.

Writing Roles

Specific activities related to the writing task were explored previously. Roles that do not merit authorship credit should also be enumerated. ICMJE guidelines provide insight. For the ICMJE, "Examples of activities that alone (without other contributions) do not qualify a contributor for authorship are acquisition of funding; general supervision of a research group or general administrative support; writing assistance, technical editing, language editing, and proofreading."[4] Similarly, the 14 CRediT (Contributor Roles Taxonomy)[5] roles put forth by the US National Information Standards Organization (NISO) include a variety of contributions that merit acknowledgment such as conceptualization, data curation, funding acquisition, and others. If the broader criteria of authorship are not met, however, these CRediT roles will not lead to inclusion in the byline and the associated authorship credit.

Non-credited writing roles include both *developmental editing* (also called author's editors[6] or, in focusing on mechanics, writing coaching) and *copyediting*. Developmental editing takes place earlier in the writing process and considers the big picture of the work, including the way the flow of ideas is presented.[7] Developmental editing includes the kinds of feedback an author might receive from the editor of their book, their writing coach through the university writing services office, or their dissertation committee chair and members. After a text is established, copyeditors revise to ensure clarity and consistency while also addressing problems relating to spelling and other elements often associated with the use of a particular style guide (e.g., hyphenation, italics, numbers and numerals). They may also work with awkward phrasing to revise for readability and will work to create a clear and consistent approach to presenting ideas throughout the text.[8] Both kinds of editing are skilled, though the work is often not acknowledged[9] and is largely invisible.[10] As with other support tasks, many writing support tasks including editing can be (and regularly are) enhanced by the use of AI. A non-human entity, AI cannot meet the requirements of authorship as laid out by the ICMJE or address the CRediT roles put forth by NISO.

Research Roles

Before anything can be written and published, some kind of research activity has to take place. Not all research is carried out by the researchers who go on to write up the work and publish it. Any number of related tasks can be considered. For example, research to identify relevant literature, coding, and work with data such as transcript cleaning can all be considered as kinds of research support.[11] Research support is often the kind of work that gives junior scholars deep experience with the research process. Menial tasks that are repetitive but that require a bit of skill such as formatting references are not particularly glamorous (if anything in the research process is), but they are necessary to the success of the project in a fundamental way. Be it through trained assistants who are paid hourly, or senior scholars themselves doing the work, the most basic research tasks must be executed with precision and care.

Increasingly, not all mundane work associated with research support is carried out by human actors. For example, researchers at Massachusetts Institute of Technology (MIT) report using AI assistants to switch off a digital gas valve at night, allowing human researchers to attend to other things.[12] Writing code is another way that AI can help humans to free themselves from mundane research support tasks.[13] By having AI-powered tools at their disposal, researchers of all levels are free to spend their time in more creative, less rote endeavors.[14]

Publishing Roles

Academic publishers help scholars participate in scholarly communication by supporting the tenets of scholarship and the requirements of authorship. At its most basic, scholarly publishing adds value by 1) choosing materials for publication, 2) providing editorial services, 3) making work available publicly, and 4) marketing it.[15] Support for creating a high-quality output includes working with editors and editorial boards, providing infrastructure, and providing writing support, but also support for creating the layout and other aspects of enduring importance to the permanent scholarly record. It is obvious that publishers allow for publication, but they also allow for legal aspects to be overseen and for libraries to be involved in acquisitions; they procure DOIs and ISBNs, they manage author rights, they expose the work to indexes and databases, they license and sell physical and digital copies, and they generally serve as gatekeepers to the pieces and stewards of the knowledge.

As with the other kinds of support of the scholarly communication process, many of these aspects of scholarly publishing can be performed in some way or another by AI.

Entering the Scholarly Record

As scholars prepare their work for publication, they work in tandem with publishers to ensure its quality and publishability. For inclusion in the scholarly record under their brand, publishers seek content that is sound and, ultimately, that is trustworthy.

Selecting High-Quality Content: Peer Review

Publishers are responsible for procedures that ensure the accuracy of materials that enter the scholarly record. One of the quintessential ways this is carried out is through the review of draft manuscripts by the author's peers. With journal articles that are peer-reviewed, once the journal's editor decides that a manuscript is worthy of consideration, that article will be sent to reviewers in the field. Reviewing the writing also puts publishers in a place to warrant, based on the assurances of experts who function as peer-reviewers, the correct and accurate presentation of content. As Michael Seadle points out, however, "peer review was never meant to be a fraud detection system per se, but a means of measuring the quality of an article."[16]

Indeed, peer review has been considered deeply flawed, in part because not all authorial mistakes will be caught, and in part because the process is subjective. For this, "even when functioning at its best, the reliability and effectiveness of peer review depend on the availability, attentiveness, and objectively of reviewers in the relevant field."[17] Yet a better solution has not been put forth. Depending on the journal, there are even possibilities for authors to game the system. In instances where names of potential reviewers are solicited by journals, unscrupulous authors can provide fake reviewers, give a fake email address that they control, and provide a glowing review of their own manuscript under a false name.[18]

Many phases of the scholarly publishing process can make use of AI-powered services, and peer review is one that invites consideration. In the section covering the publisher-related "Responsibilities in the Submission and Peer-Review Process," the ICMJE provides information regarding peer review and AI. In terms of related obligations for journals, AI (presumably AI-powered chatbots like ChatGPT) as a tool to process manuscripts is described as potentially violating confidentiality, and its use is implied to be best avoided. A journal's instructions for reviewers should, according to the ICMJE, include a warning against the use of such AI-powered tools.[19] In regard to peer reviewers and AI, the ICMJE further recommends that peer reviewers bear in mind concerns about confidentiality and seek permission from the journal prior to uploading manuscripts under review to AI-powered tools.[20]

Preparing the Manuscript for Publication

For works of adequate intellectual quality, publishers support improvements in the manuscripts they accept for publication and that they will distribute in the future. In the interest of protecting intellectual property, publishers are able to enforce author's securing of permissions to re-use previously published or otherwise protected content that they did not develop themselves. They can also anticipate how best to ensure that authors receive proper credit, often through the inclusion of an ORCID identifier for the author as a way to disambiguate authors with identical names.

Copyeditors employed by the publisher complete the manuscript's preparation; the work being intertwined with that of the author because

> the copyeditor must often perform functions that the author has neglected, and because the author's responsibilities for preparing the manuscript are not fully met until he or she has responded to the editing and answered all queries on the manuscript.[21]

Finding errors, ensuring the correctness and accuracy of citations and references, and generally ensuring the logic and flow of a piece can all be part of the work of copyeditors. Again, much of this work can now be automated, or at the very least supplemented by technology.

Publishers also oversee the way a manuscript is laid out. Although word processing software has allowed authors to seamlessly combine elements of word processing (i.e., work with text) and other elements of pay layout including headings, columns, and the integration of tables and images and their titles and captions can also be done through word processors.[22] In scholarly publishing, however, academic publishers must oversee the formatting and layout of accepted content rather than leaving such an important part of their brand to authors.

Establishing the Version of Record

Publishers go to great lengths to make sure the final version of a piece is as flawless as possible on all counts, and their duties are upheld. Once established, the version of record for articles will not be modified, ensuring the integrity of the piece and the traceability over time of the flow of ideas. Any new versions of the work will need to be substantially different in terms of intellectual content or risk self-plagiarism. For conference proceedings moving to join the scholarly record as articles, the rule of thumb is the addition of around 30% new content and transparency about the original proceedings; for books this means content added or removed.[23] The version of record becomes a trustworthy and enduring legacy of the authors, and evidence of the quality of the work that was carried out.

Protecting Intellectual Property Rights

Authors participate in the "dangers of writing" potentially leaving themselves legally accountable for the content they produce. In the process, they are "conferred the benefits of property."[24] These benefits include the benefits the academy bestows on authors and the prestige academics accord each other based on their work. Given the paltry economic value of individual instances of academic writing, the authors and their institutions are likely not interested in enforcing legal ownership rights. For authors who might not be expert in managing these rights, their rights can be signed over to publishers who will secure the content; unfortunately for authors without the funds to support open access, the assertion of rights by the publisher might lead to their piece being unavailable to readers and hidden behind a "firewall."

The rights owner can enforce ownership privileges, including use and reuse of the resource. The owner of the intellectual content also has the right to make money or not, and can indicate who can use the content and how. Since authors are not making money from their scholarship, they may feel strongly that their work should be accessible to the largest possible number of potential readers. The copyleft movement and Creative Commons provide owners of intellectual content with approaches for making the work accessible while potentially limiting the ways it can be used, reused, and redistributed – an idea that aligns very well with ideals of universalism. Unfortunately for junior faculty, open approaches can minimize perceptions of quality, and very unfairly so, at the same time diminishing prestige and authority.[25] When publishing through standards publishers, authors can make their work open access, freely allowing it to be consumed by those with a web connection.

All of this means that today, authors are considered "as owners with enduring rights to their work"[26] whether the publisher holds the copyright, whether they do, or whether the work is in the public domain. When content is taken from them in a way that is unethical, however, as through plagiarism or through the unauthorized use of the piece for training AI, a host of new ethical questions emerges.

Ethical Concerns for Scholarship

Both human actors and computers contribute to the ethical enactment of scholarly communication practices. The field of machine ethics is well developed, and unsurprisingly, many of the concerns relating to AI ethics can have an impact on research and writing in scholarly contexts, and seem to echo longstanding concerns about human actors' engagement. Nick Bostrom and Eliezer Yudkowsky identify a series of ethical concerns relating to AI that must nonetheless be addressed but yet that are not frequently discussed in the technical literature. Their concerns arise because "when AI algorithms take on cognitive work with social dimensions – cognitive tasks previously performed by humans – the AI algorithm inherits the social requirements."[27] Some concerns include the requirement that AI be transparent to inspection (i.e., opening the black box), that output be predictable, that it be robust against manipulation, and that a responsible individual be answerable to problems that arise from its use.

All of these concerns relate to the work of scholars and their use of AI in research and writing. Of the possible abuses of the responsibilities of scholars as they pertain to carrying out and presenting their work, misconduct is particularly devastating. Generally speaking, misconduct takes place when the social contract that is academic integrity is not respected; from the perspective of authorship, misconduct allows the author to reap benefits of authorship that have not been earned. A student using a paper mill to author a term paper, a senior faculty submitting his junior colleague's work as his own, a journal article reviewer taking text or ideas from a manuscript she evaluated, or a tenure-track faculty member falsifying his publication record to seem as if he had published more are all examples of academic misconduct. In all of these cases, responsibilities of authorship are not met, but the benefits of authorship are claimed. As with other behaviors that are not socially tolerated, like cutting in line at the bank or grocery store, some violate our social code but are not illegal. All of them, potentially, could bring harm to the enduring scholarly record.

In the assessment of effects of misconduct on the part of the research community, COPE identifies a series of harms. These include concerns related to loss of trust in the products of scholarly communication; harms to collaborators, colleagues, and institutions who did not have a hand in the misconduct; and distortion of the scholarly record. If undetected, flawed work could become part of the scholarly record, potentially shaping both policy and future funding priorities.[28] The types of misconduct identified by COPE that are most germane to discussions of both authorship and AI are 1) fabrication; 2) falsification, including image manipulation; 3) plagiarism; 4) selective reporting; 5) inappropriate authorship; and 6) undeclared conflicts of interests.[29] The first three types of misconduct fall under the umbrella of *research misconduct* or *research fraud* and were already classified as *fraud* by sociologist of science Robert K. Merton in 1950.[30] Since 2000, the US Office of Science and Technology Policy (OSTP)[31] has led the way in defining these three practices with other US federal agencies adopting their approach as the Federal Policy on Research Misconduct.[32] In scholarly journals, these three practices have been euphemistically termed *questionable research practices*[33] in part because of the socially constructed nature of the perception of the actions. Each generation of scholars seems to find that the current environment presents risks and is particularly ripe for abuse (e.g., AI is now permitting abuses at a scale never before imagined).[34] No matter one's perception, however, misconduct is nonetheless no less potentially deleterious to the scholarly record.

Fabrication

Of the COPE examples of authorship misconduct, "Fabrication is making up data or results and recording or reporting them."[35] This first in the COPE list of research fraud examples is perhaps the most odious due to the intentionality required; it is also possibly the most sensational when caught. One of the most notorious academics brought down over data fabrication and data manipulation is Diederik Stapel, Dutch professor of social psychology. Stapel is infamous for creating data whole cloth and publishing the resulting work in well-respected journals. Not merely content to put his own career in danger, he would also hand over fabricated or massaged data to his doctoral students for analysis, including for their own dissertation research.[36]

Such breaches of trust are indeed sensational when they come to light, and fortunately, such cases are uncommon. Trust that has been lost is difficult to regain, however, which might provide insight into another of the reasons that fabrication is often listed first among the examples of research misconduct.

Falsification and Selective Reporting

"Falsification is manipulating research materials, equipment, or processes, or changing or omitting data or results such that the research is not accurately represented in the research record"[37] Falsification, as a kind of misconduct, ostensibly involves data that has been legitimately collected but that in some way is does not meet expectations; with a bit of "housekeeping," it will be made to be more publishable. Specifically, COPE considers *selective reporting* to be "when unfavourable or inconvenient end-points (e.g. outcomes that fail to reach statistical significance or do not favour a particular product or hypothesis) are deliberately omitted from publications reporting research."[38] The real-world example that Neil C. Herndon gives in an editorial in the *Journal of Marketing Channels* is of an ambitious associate professor who would meticulously "sanitize" their data by removing inconvenient results, leading to publications in top journals. This person is now, according to Herndon, a successful senior scholar in a chair professorship.[39] Of the 3,247 early and mid-career researchers in the US surveyed by Brian C. Martinson and colleagues, 6% of respondents admitted to failing to present data that contradicted their previous work, which is another example of selective reporting of results.[40]

Plagiarism

Plagiarism is defined by the US government as "the appropriation of another person's ideas, processes, results, or words without giving appropriate credit."[41] To plagiarize is an act of research fraud that obscures the scholarly record, potentially confusing priority claims and breaking the intellectual connections to previous works for subsequent pieces. Put another way, plagiarism is a form of intellectual theft of the ideas or words created by another. As a result, the scholarly record is stripped of its ability to capture the flow of ideas accurately, to reward priority claims, and to see scholars earn the accolades they deserve. The obverse is also true, as responsible parties cannot be held responsible, in the case of problematic research, if the authors of the work are not acknowledged.

All three kinds of misconduct mentioned here are particularly susceptible to being carried out through chatbots like ChatGPT. AI-powered systems exude (anthropomorphized) intelligence but are, in fact, black boxes prone to fabrication, falsification, and plagiarism.

Inappropriate Authorship and Undeclared Conflicts of Interests

Transparency in terms of authorship is an essential part of the scholarly communication process, and one that can be obscured through the use of chatbots like ChatGPT. Authorship-related misconduct involving both inappropriate authorship and undeclared conflicts of interest[42] is problematic. Martinson and colleagues found that 10% of over 3,000 early and mid-career researchers surveyed had inappropriately assigned authorship credit.[43]

The name on the byline of a scholarly or creative work is meant to be reflective of the extent of contributions of all human actors, but this is not always the case. For example, the extent to which quid quo pro authorship takes place is always likely underreported. In quid pro quo authorship, inclusion on a byline is advantageous for both the author and the individual receiving the credit, because both parties benefit – presenting itself as a *victimless crime* that tends to go unreported.[44] Yet the scholarly record is marred by the inability of the *guest* to meet authorship criteria, and the scholarly community is held to standards of inflated authorship credit.

Conflicts of interest can manifest between authors and external actors as well. Of the over researchers surveyed by Martinson and colleagues, 1.4% had questionable relationships with students, research subjects, or clients, and 15.5% had changed some aspect of a study due to pressure from funders.[45] Both of these scenarios present as conflicts of interest, possibly negatively influencing the research as presented. Combined, the two types of misconduct are found in certain cases of ghost authorship. As an example, pharmaceutical companies have been criticized for deploying ghostwriters to partner with respected academics on research, with the potential for the presentation of the results to be abused to the benefit of the company.[46]

Unethical Publishing Practices

Authors are not the only actors in the scholarly communication ecosystem who might commit misconduct. COPE[47] considers that editors, reviewers, publishers, and funders might all take part in activities that are considered to be examples of misconduct. According to COPE, the kinds of misconduct on the part of those involved in the publishing process might include plagiarism and undisclosed conflicts of interest. For example, if in their own work, a peer reviewer uses content that was encountered through the evaluation of a manuscript, citing that unpublished work is not sufficient, the act is an act of misconduct. This represents a case of theft of intellectual content, or plagiarism, and is considered research misconduct.

Actors in the publishing process can also block meritorious work in other ways. For example, for any number of reasons unrelated to the legitimacy of the work, foot-dragging and slow responses from editors or reviewers might discourage authors from following through in seeking publication. As well, biased assessments unrelated to the intellectual merits of the work could block manuscripts from consideration or publication. Negative assessments could reflect preconceived notions about particular authors or classes of authors from certain institutions, countries, or fields, including the specific topics they choose to explore.[48] Discounting work categorically, based on the authors or their backgrounds or specific geographically related interests, deprives the larger scholarly community of the opportunity to be enriched by their work. Such an approach, whether intentional or not, diminishes the trustworthiness of the scholarly record as a whole.[49]

Ethical Ambiguities and Blurred Lines

Misconduct is narrowly defined by publishers, funding agencies, and employers, but their interpretation of these phenomena is nonetheless a snapshot in time from a very specific perspective. Other dubious approaches to scholarship can put the scholarly record at equal risk even if they are not considered to be "misconduct" per the US federal policy. Examples include what COPE considers to be "unethical research" such as flouting requirements for work with human subjects or abusing access to confidential information for research purposes.[50] These, along with inadequate record keeping, were also mentioned by Martinson and colleagues as problematic areas per their survey.[51]

Ultimately, some behaviors are unethical because they clearly violate the norms of science as well as other social perceptions of right versus wrong, but that is not always the case, and social perceptions of right and wrong can vary greatly. Not everything is so cut and dried, despite the messaging that is put forth.

Even when considering narrow definitions of misconduct or fraud, some approaches consider that the actions must be intentional; that means that *mens rea*, which is Latin for "guilty mind," must be a factor. This approach distinguishes plagiarism where citations are intentionally withheld from sloppy work. Fraud in both the form of intentional theft and unintended lapses in ethics due to carelessness affect the scholarly record by not appropriately crediting sources, and both are equally sanctioned under the US federal policy but not necessarily across the board.

Disciplinary differences affect how work is presented, which can also have a bearing on perceptions of its ethical enactment. From an authorship standpoint, for example, in some disciplines an expectation might exist for students to include their advisor as a coauthor since the advisor would have helped with the conceptualizing of a piece.[52] For example, a lab supervisor might claim "senior author" or last author position on a paper on which they did not work, simply because the research took place in their lab or otherwise made use of resources they had procured. Such *guest* or *honorary authorship* can be extraordinarily meaningful professionally, especially in disciplines where last author status is coveted for senior scholars and in institutions where a certain number of publications are required for continued appointment. All told, the bylines of articles do not systematically tell a story about the degree of involvement of each person listed there, potentially opening the scholarly record to such abuses.

International Considerations for Authorship Activities

Challenges to a consistent approach across the scholarly record are also affected by cultural differences that confound a consistent, one-size-fits-all approach to presenting work. In terms of authorship designation, as described earlier, differing practices regarding authorship practices may emerge in particular fields or disciplines.[53] Internationally, similar practices can be identified by country or geographical region, for example, where junior scholars are tolerant of adding senior colleagues to the bylines of their work due to a flawed interpretation of the "substantial contributions" brought by individuals of power who did not directly participate in the research.[54]

Differing cultural approaches to text ownership and the attribution of ideas in scholarship have been well documented in the literature, with scholars from Eastern and post-soviet countries, for example, generally being seen to have more collectivist approaches to intellectual property.[55] Scholars may even find themselves in research environments where plagiarism, as defined in the Western tradition described here, is not only tolerated; it is the norm.[56] Ultimately, what is termed misconduct in some traditions might be acceptable behavior in others. Generally, the Anglo-Western European approach is considered to be the most stringent, even if, in reality, these scholars might not be much more virtuous than their Eastern European, Asian, and African counterparts.[57]

Authorship in the Era of AI-Powered Systems

In 1942, Robert K. Merton laid out four norms undergirding the ethos of science as it had evolved over the course of the previous several hundred years.[58]

These principles have informed approaches to scholarship since. Building trust in the scholarly record requires agency and accountability on the part of authors, which is something that systems like ChatGPT at present do not allow. "Generative AI is new and requires a reset of the current standards of practice in scientific inquiry and publication so that they are inclusive of the breadth available to individuals because of the easy accessibility of AI."[59] In other words, although AI has been around for quite a long time, the polemics that are arising, linked to the concern about the future of the scholarly record, are most tightly aligned with chatbots like ChatGPT that are easy to access and use but that do not allow for the level of accountability and ethical enactment needed to ensure trust in the scholarly record. Alas, *writing with intelligence* at present still requires authors to write *intelligently*, on their own, but is increasingly including partnerships with AI-powered systems where the computer's work is carefully overseen by the scholar.

The next chapter explores the different historical approaches to AI, culminating in the technologies that have enabled systems like ChatGPT to explode onto the scholarly communication scene in recent years.

Notes

1 Rick Anderson, *Scholarly Communication: What Everyone Needs to Know, What Everyone Needs to Know* (New York, NY: Oxford University Press, 2018).
2 ICMJE, "Defining the Role of Authors and Contributors," *A, Sec. 2. Who Is an Author?*, para. 1, https://www.icmje.org/recommendations/browse/roles-and-responsibilities/defining-the-role-of-authors-and-contributors.html.
3 ICMJE, "Defining the Role of Authors and Contributors."
4 ICMJE, "Defining the Role of Authors and Contributors," *Sec. 3. Non-Author Contributors*, para. 1.
5 NISO (National Information Standards Organization), "Contributor Role Taxonomy (CRediT)," *CRediT*, accessed December 12, 2024, https://credit.niso.org/.
6 Karen Shashok, "Author's Editors: Facilitators of Science Information Transfer," *Learned Publishing* 14, no. 2 (2001): 113–21, https://doi.org/10.1087/095315101300059495.
7 Lourdes Venard, "What Is Copyediting? And How Does It Differ from Proofreading? | Continuing Education | UC San Diego Division of Extended Studies," September 6, 2023, https://extendedstudies.ucsd.edu/news-and-events/blog/what-is-copyediting-and-how-does-it-differ-from-proofreading.
8 Simon Dunton and Audrey D. Melkin, "Are Copy Editors an Endangered Species?," *Learned Publishing* 16, no. 4 (2003): 309–15, https://doi.org/10.1087/095315103322422062; Venard, "What Is Copyediting?"
9 Robert Brown, "How Scholars Credit Editors in Their Acknowledgements," *Journal of Scholarly Publishing* 40, no. 4 (June 2009): 384–98, https://doi.org/10.3138/jsp.40.4.384; Sylvia Hunter, "Why Copy Editors Matter," *Journal of Scholarly Publishing* 36, no. 1 (October 2004): 6–14, https://doi.org/10.3138/jsp.36.1.6.

10 Hunter, "Why Copy Editors Matter."
11 Smit Desai and Michael Twidale, "Using Playful Metaphors to Conceptualize Practical Use of ChatGPT: An Autoethnography," *Proceedings of the Association for Information Science and Technology* 60, no. 1 (2023): 565–69, https://doi.org/10.1002/pra2.816.
12 Poornima Apte, "Accelerating Research with AI-Assisted Experiments," *MIT Department of Materials Science and Engineering* (blog), December 20, 2023, https://dmse.mit.edu/news/accelerating-research-with-ai-assisted-experiments/.
13 Mustafa Suleyman, *The Coming Wave: Technology, Power, and the Twenty-First Century's Greatest Dilemma*, 1st ed. (New York: Crown, 2023).
14 Jennifer Chubb, Peter Cowling, and Darren Reed, "Speeding up to Keep up: Exploring the Use of AI in the Research Process," *AI & Society* 37, no. 4 (December 1, 2022): 1439–57, https://doi.org/10.1007/s00146-021-01259-0.
15 Anderson, *Scholarly Communication*.
16 Michael Seadle, "Fake Reviewers," *iSchools*, December 10, 2024, para. 3, https://www.ischools.org/so/edPEhoC1J?languageTag=en.
17 Anderson, *Scholarly Communication*, 67.
18 Neil C. Herndon, "Research Fraud and the Publish or Perish World of Academia," *Journal of Marketing Channels* 23, no. 3 (July 2, 2016): 91–96, https://doi.org/10.1080/1046669X.2016.1186469.
19 ICMJE, "Responsibilities in the Submission and Peer-Review Process," *B, Sec. 2*, https://www.icmje.org/recommendations/browse/roles-and-responsibilities/responsibilities-in-the-submission-and-peer-peview-process.html.
20 ICMJE, "Responsibilities in the Submission and Peer-Review Process."
21 *The Chicago Manual of Style*, 14th ed. (Chicago: University of Chicago Press, 1993), 49.
22 Amanda Presley, "What Is Desktop Publishing and How Does It Differ from Word Processing?," January 28, 2010, https://www.brighthub.com/multimedia/publishing/articles/62697/.
23 Bowker, "FAQs: Publication Formats, Reprints, Editions, Etc.," *Text, ISBN.org*, 2024, https://www.isbn.org/faqs_formats_reprints_editions.
24 Michel Foucault, "What Is an Author?," in *Language, Counter-Memory, Practice*, ed. Donald F. Bouchard, trans. Donald F. Bouchard and Sherry Simon (Ithaca, NY: Cornell University Press, 1977), 125.
25 Peter Suber, *Open Access, MIT Press Essential Knowledge Series* (Cambridge, MA: MIT Press, 2012).
26 Mary Carruthers, *The Book of Memory: A Study of Memory in Medieval Culture*, 2nd ed. (Cambridge, UK and New York: Cambridge University Press, 2008), 273.
27 Nick Bostrom and Eliezer Yudkowsky, "The Ethics of Artificial Intelligence," in *The Cambridge Handbook of Artificial Intelligence*, ed. Keith Frankish and William M. Ramsey (Cambridge, UK: Cambridge University Press, 2014), 317, http://assets.cambridge.org/97805218/71426/cover/9780521871426.jpg.
28 COPE: Committee on Publication Ethics, "Why Should You Be Concerned?," *Introduction to Publication Ethics*, 2024, https://publicationethics.org/resources/elearning/introduction-publication-ethics/why-should-you-be-concerned.

29 COPE: Committee on Publication Ethics, "Why Should You Be Concerned?"
30 Robert K. Merton, "Priorities in Scientific Discovery: A Chapter in the Sociology of Science," *American Sociological Review* 22, no. 6 (December 1957): 635, https://doi.org/10.2307/2089193.
31 For example, https://www.whitehouse.gov/ostp/.
32 For example, Nicholas H. Steneck, *Introduction to the Responsible Conduct of Research* (ORI (Office of Research Integrity), August 2007), https://ori.hhs.gov/ori-introduction-responsible-conduct-research.
33 Herndon, "Research Fraud and the Publish or Perish World of Academia."
34 For example, Debra Jackson et al., "Multiple Outputs from Single Studies: Acceptable Division of Findings vs. 'Salami' Slicing," *Journal of Clinical Nursing* 23, no. 1–2 (January 2014): 1–2, https://doi.org/10.1111/jocn.12439.
35 ORI – The Office of Research Integrity, "Office of Science and Technology Policy Federal Policy on Research Misconduct," accessed October 22, 2024, https://ori.hhs.gov/content/chapter-2-research-misconduct-office-science-and-technology-policy.
36 John M. Budd, "The Stapel Case: An Object Lesson in Research Integrity and Its Lapses," *Synesis: A Journal of Science, Technology, Ethics, and Policy* 4 (2013): G:47–G:53.
37 ORI – The Office of Research Integrity, "Office of Science and Technology Policy Federal Policy on Research Misconduct."
38 COPE: Committee on Publication Ethics, "Why Should You Be Concerned?"
39 Herndon, "Research Fraud and the Publish or Perish World of Academia."
40 Brian C. Martinson, Melissa S. Anderson, and Raymond de Vries, "Scientists Behaving Badly," *Nature* 435, no. 7043 (June 2005): 737–38, https://doi.org/10.1038/435737a.
41 ORI – The Office of Research Integrity, "Office of Science and Technology Policy Federal Policy on Research Misconduct."
42 COPE: Committee on Publication Ethics, "Why Should You Be Concerned?"
43 Martinson, Anderson, and de Vries, "Scientists Behaving Badly."
44 Devon Whetstone, Laura Ridenour, and Heather Moulaison-Sandy, "Quid Pro Quo Authorship: Characteristics and Implications," *Journal of Scholarly Publishing* 54, no. 1 (January 1, 2023): 15–29, https://doi.org/10.3138/jsp-2022-0035.
45 Martinson, Anderson, and de Vries, "Scientists Behaving Badly."
46 For example, Drummond Rennie and Annette Flanagin, "Authorship! Authorship!: Guests, Ghosts, Grafters, and the Two-Sided Coin," *Journal of the American Medical Association* 271, no. 6 (1994): 469–71.
47 COPE: Committee on Publication Ethics, "Why Should You Be Concerned?"
48 In 2016, a survey by publisher Taylor & Francis seemed to indicate that biases were suspected on the part of authors, reviewers, and editors. Herndon, "Research Fraud and the Publish or Perish World of Academia."
49 Other forms of manipulation have also emerged, with accounts of authors hacking journal databases or setting up citation rings to inflate their citations, and with accounts of journal editors setting up citation rings

to inflate the rankings of their journals. Mario Biagioli and Alexandra Lippman, "Introduction: Metrics and the New Ecologies of Academic Misconduct," in *Gaming the Metrics: Misconduct and Manipulation in Academic Research*, ed. Mario Biagioli and Alexandra Lippman (The MIT Press, 2020), 2, https://doi.org/10.7551/mitpress/11087.001.0001.

50 COPE: Committee on Publication Ethics, "Why Should You Be Concerned?"

51 Martinson, Anderson, and de Vries, "Scientists Behaving Badly."

52 For example, Neil C. Herndon, "Research Fraud and the Publish or Perish World of Academia," *Journal of Marketing Channels* 23, no. 3 (July 2, 2016): 91–96, https://doi.org/10.1080/1046669X.2016.1186469.

53 For example, Maureen Shawn Kennedy, Jane Barnsteiner, and John Daly, "Honorary and Ghost Authorship in Nursing Publications," *Journal of Nursing Scholarship* 46, no. 6 (2014): 416–22, https://doi.org/10.1111/jnu.12093.

54 Mads Paludan Goddiksen et al., "'The Person in Power Told Me to' – European PhD Students' Perspectives on Guest Authorship and Good Authorship Practice," *PLoS One* 18, no. 1 (January 12, 2023): e0280018, https://doi.org/10.1371/journal.pone.0280018; Priya Satalkar, Thomas Perneger, and David Shaw, "Accommodating an Uninvited Guest: Perspectives of Researchers in Switzerland on 'Honorary' Authorship," *Science and Engineering Ethics* 26, no. 2 (April 1, 2020): 947–67, https://doi.org/10.1007/s11948-019-00162-8.

55 Dawn Amsberry, "Deconstructing Plagiarism: International Students and Textual Borrowing Practices," *The Reference Librarian* 51, no. 1 (December 21, 2009): 31–44, https://doi.org/10.1080/02763870903362183.

56 Elizabeth Heitman and Sergio Litewka, "International Perspectives on Plagiarism and Considerations for Teaching International Trainees," *Urologic Oncology* 29, no. 1 (2011): 104–8, https://doi.org/10.1016/j.urolonc.2010.09.014.

57 David C. Ison, "An Empirical Analysis of Differences in Plagiarism Among World Cultures," *Journal of Higher Education Policy and Management* 40, no. 4 (July 4, 2018): 291–304, https://doi.org/10.1080/1360080X.2018.1479949.

58 Robert K. Merton, "The Normative Structure of Science, 1942," in *The Sociology of Science: Theoretical and Empirical Investigations* (Chicago: University of Chicago Press, 1973), 267–78, http://archive.org/details/robert_K_merton_the_sociology_of_science.

59 Ellen Chetwynd, "Ethical Use of Artificial Intelligence for Scientific Writing: Current Trends," *Journal of Human Lactation* 40, no. 2 (May 2024): 211, https://doi.org/10.1177/08903344241235160.

3 AI Technologies and Scholarly Communication

Artificial intelligence (AI) is shorthand for the technologies and approaches that allow computational systems to engage with content in a way that approximates how humans would, if indeed humans had the capacity of computers for analyzing vast quantities of data. The future of AI envisions a complete replication of general human intellectual abilities termed artificial general intelligence (AGI). That future has not yet arrived, but the AI in use today is making strides.

In scholarly communication, current AI systems play out most readily in terms of the way they support the work of the researcher and author, but also how they can understand the work of the publisher, peer reviewer, copyeditor, and others involved in creating a high-quality scholarly record. Indeed, today's AI is best applied in limited environments, specifically summarized by Sheela Kolluri and colleagues as ones where:

- Data are cheap
- Success and failure are obvious
- Rules are explicit
- Tasks are repetitive[1]

This chapter focuses on the kinds of AI that are most readily involved in supporting scholarly communication, itself a limited environment but with well-established standards and practices. Although some aspects of scholarship might meet requirements mentioned by Kolluri and colleagues, many others emphatically will not.

Three phases are often identified with the development of AI since the second half of the past century: 1) expert systems from the 1970s, 2) machine learning beginning around 1980, and 3) deep learning which took off around 2010.[2] Mirroring that approach, this chapter begins with a discussion of the first two phases of AI, expert systems and machine learning, and concludes with a focus on the deep learning phase that has wrought the likes of ChatGPT and DALL-E, with a particular focus on how such systems might impact scholarship and scholarly communication.

DOI: 10.4324/9781003570325-3

Expert Systems

The first phase of AI generally identified that *expert systems* simulate human judgments or behavior in very specific scenarios based on a knowledge base. Using an inference or rules engine, they apply what is provided in the knowledge base to the question at hand. Users access expert systems through a user interface. Although not meant to replace human experts, expert systems can mimic human experts, and like human experts, they can continue to learn.[3] One familiar expert system might be a financial advisor tool that provides investment recommendations based on client responses to a questionnaire; another example might be customer service chatbots like Kik that help online customers understand products.

One thing to note is the use of the term "chatbot" in this context. Indeed, chatbots have been around for a very long time. "A chatbot can be any software/system that holds dialogue with you/a person but doesn't necessarily have to be AI-powered. For example, there are chatbots that are rules-based in the sense that they'll give canned responses to questions."[4] Specialized chatbots have long been used in specific environments, including in libraries.[5] As AI technology has improved, chatbots have likewise advanced, meaning that today's generation of AI-powered chatbots incorporates advanced AI technologies. These systems are not infallible though and will depend heavily on the data used to train them. One example of a special-purpose AI-powered chatbot that was shut down in 2023 is Tessa, the US National Eating Disorders Association's chatbot, which started giving advice that promoted disordered eating behaviors.[6] As a kind of best-case scenario, interacting with ChatGPT will be a very different experience from a session with ELIZA, one of the first chatbots made available in the 1960s and the one associated with passing the Turing test in light of the AI technologies used, it will also be a very different experience from getting help with a merchandise return through Amazon's automated chatbot system.

Machine Learning (ML)

After expert systems, the next phase of AI often invoked is the *machine learning* (ML) phase. Going beyond the ability to look up answers in a knowledge base and to guide users as a human expert might, ML "is a subset of AI associated with providing machines the ability to learn from experience without the need to be programmed explicitly."[7] In other words, after they are trained on appropriate datasets, ML systems use algorithms to detect and predict patterns.[8] With ML able to generate new information, predicted based on what was learned, it is useful in the research process and beyond since ML can make predictions, classify objects, cluster data, and detect patterns based on data. Familiar examples of ML include fraud detection in banking and the self-driving aspects of autonomous vehicles. ML can also include recommendation engines like Netflix's movie recommendation stream and speech recognition capabilities in virtual assistants like Alexa. Specifically, when tasks focus on extracting information from images or video rather than text, which is generally called *computer vision*.[9] Apple's Face ID recognition system is an example of computer vision.

ML is often classified as being either *supervised* or *unsupervised*. Supervised (machine) learning requires a labeled dataset. For example, in the field of computer vision if a system is being trained to identify images of dogs and to differentiate them from images of cats, the training data will need to include labeled images of each.[10] The difference between supervised and unsupervised is important in research when considering how biases might inadvertently be integrated. One example is the story that Liz O'Sullivan tells, where an ML system was being developed to identify obscene images on the internet. To train the system, a set of images was sent to India, where workers labeled explicit photos as indecent, but also innocuous images of same-sex couples, introducing an unintended bias into the training data.[11]

Unsupervised (machine) learning, instead "uses machine learning (ML) algorithms to analyze and cluster unlabeled data sets. These algorithms discover hidden patterns or data groupings without the need for human intervention."[12] One example that has been applied in scholarship is *topic modeling*, a kind of unsupervised (machine) learning technique that does not need to train on pre-labeled categories of data.[13] Specifically, "[t]opic modelling generally uses a process called 'latent Dirichlet allocation' (LDA) to cluster terms that probabilistically co-occur in similar contexts."[14] Topic modeling is used in research that seeks to make meaning from large text-based corpora, including ones that investigate social media,[15] information retrieval,[16] entire fields of study,[17] and text-based summaries of documents.[18]

Natural Language Processing (NLP)

Natural language processing (NLP) services analyze, understand, and generate human language, enabling services such as sentiment analysis, text summarization, and speech recognition. Although NLP does not necessarily have to make use of ML, the aforementioned services do; they also focus on human language, which is important when considering NLP.

NLP-based products have been in use for a long time, including in email filtering and spam detection systems, machine translation systems, and speech recognition systems. Many if not all of these will be familiar to scholars, as all of them can be used as part of their work. Editorial tasks, including sentence completion, autocorrect, spellcheck, and others integrated in word processors and authoring assistants, are common examples of NLP systems used by authors in scholarly writing and that can be used as well throughout the scholarly publishing process.

Deep Learning (DL)

The third phase of AI is generally considered to be *deep learning* (DL). DL is much more recent than expert systems and ML, having first emerged around 2010. DL is a subset of ML[19] that is designed to "simulate the complex decision-making power of the human brain."[20] DL has moved the field of AI forward very quickly, at a time when it had all but stalled out. Now, many of the AI-powered systems available are examples of DL systems. A number of deep learning models exist, with the one most relevant to text-based production being the transformer models.

Transformer models were introduced in 2017 and are integral to a variety of AI systems, including ChatGPT.

> OpenAI's popular ChatGPT text generation tool makes use of transformer architectures for prediction, summarization, question answering and more, because they allow the model to focus on the most relevant segments of input text. The "GPT" seen in the tool's various versions (e.g. GPT-2, GPT-3) stands for "generative pre-trained transformer." Text-based generative AI tools such as ChatGPT benefit from transformer models because they can more readily predict the next word in a sequence of text, based on a large, complex data sets.[21]

Other kinds of DL models exist, but for the purposes of this book, the focus will be on transformer models that are behind the advancements in AI that have given way to systems like ChatGPT.

Generative AI Models

Generative AI models, or GenAI models, rely on DL models[22] and generate new data samples or content based on existing patterns or examples, enabling tasks such as image synthesis, text generation, and music composition. ChatGPT's rollout in November 2022 focused on text, but that is not to say, however, that image and sound creation are not equally exciting and important fields.

AI-powered systems to support the creation of images, including video, have been around for a number of years. The blurred backgrounds in Zoom are one example (and Zoom's ability to silence jackhammers or lawnmowers is an example of the system's ability to focus on the human voice). Although memes circulating on the web might not seem relevant to a discussion of AI and scholarly communication, they can nonetheless be instructive regarding the state of the field, its capacity to advance, and the expectations and use cases that scholars might be exploring in their free time. One example is the meme that started in 2023, with a user of the Modelscope Text2Video generator creating a somewhat disturbing video of what is supposed to be the actor Will Smith eating spaghetti.[23] These AI-powered video-creation systems have improved dramatically since then, with recognizable Will Smiths eating spaghetti more or less properly in more recent iterations.[24] Although more harmful uses of the technology have also come to light, the functionality of the systems is nonetheless quite impressive.

A similar trajectory of improvements has been seen with audio, from Alexa and Siri's understanding of a wide range of accents in English, to generating a human voice and creating music. Likewise, some of these advances have been put to nefarious uses such as the replication of a grandchild's voice used on the phone to swindle unsuspecting grandparents. These also demonstrate the state of the field, however, and the improvements that have been made in a relatively short time.

Large Language Models (LLMs)

Large language models (LLMs) are GenAI models using DL and NLP that produce text as the output. Human language and computer code tend to be the two types of text-based content most readily produced.

> The classic training exercise for an LLM is not predicting what word best describes contents of an image; It is predicting what a word cut from a piece of text is, on the basis of the other words around it.[25]

LLMs do this in a very specific way.

> In the context of Large Language Models (LLMs), the term "token" refers to a chunk of text that the model reads or generates.
>
> A token is typically not a word; it could be a smaller unit, like a character or a part of a word, or a larger one like a whole phrase.
>
> In the GPT architecture, a sequence of tokens serves as the input and/or output during both training and inference (the stage where the model generates text based on a given prompt).[26]

In order for LLMs to be able to make predictions about possible word combinations in the form of the output, massive amounts of training data are needed. That data does not need to be labeled or curated, but it does need to be copious.[27] In this way, the "large" of the large language models refers to the training data, which for many systems will include everything from Wikipedia articles to social media content.

Another way to think of LLMs is that they are carrying out a sort of text completion in response to the user's prompt. "For most models, simply asking a question or typing an instruction won't yield the best results. That's because the model isn't *answering* your prompt, the model is *appending text to it*."[28]

This aspect of LLMs has been referred to, somewhat cheekily, as "spicy autocomplete." Not unlike the autocomplete functionality that is part of many web search engines, LLMs are simply pulling together frequently combined words in the output. Considered from this perspective, this approach is very different from other ones that use NLP, in that LLMs are not attempting to *understand* the meaning of the sentences,[29] so much as predict combinations of words. "Natural language understanding (NLU) is a subset of NLP that focuses on analyzing the meaning behind sentences."[30] In their groundbreaking paper on LLMs, joint first authors Emily Bender and Timnit Gebru and colleagues demonstrate that this kind of *understanding* is not, however, the goal of LLMs.[31]

One benefit of LLMs is that they are designed to be multipurpose. LLMs are not simply working in one domain from a knowledge base, as an expert system, nor are they functioning as a domain-specific application such as ML-powered email spam filters. Rather, LLMs are able to react to user input in the form of prompts and generate language in a way that is reminiscent of a human.[32] All of this can lead to concerns about the anthropomorphized intelligence of these systems, as well as aspects obscured by the black box.

Reinforcement Learning

One way that LLMs develop such a human-like ability to produce text is through reinforcement learning (RL):

> A technique that teaches an A.I. model to find the best result by trial and error, receiving rewards or punishments from an algorithm based on its results. This system can be enhanced by humans giving feedback on its performance, in the form of ratings, corrections and suggestions.[33]

Reinforcement learning from human feedback (RLHF) engages humans to give specific feedback.[34] As with other elements of human-mediated interpretation, RL can be both very good and flawed at the same time. It nonetheless allows LLMs to interact with their users in ways that seem surprisingly human.

Emergent Behavior

Emergent behavior is one aspect of LLMs that makes them compelling to use. Unlike other systems, "if LLMs are trained on sufficiently large amounts of text data, they are capable of generating novel sequences of words never observed previously by the model, but that represent plausible sequences based on natural human language."[35] With LLMs, "[t]he basic function is to predict the next word in a sequence, but these models have surprised experts by learning new abilities."[36] Stringing together words in unanticipated ways, such as forming sonnets or other highly structured or idiosyncratic forms of language, was not anticipated but has proven to delight users.

End-User Perspectives and Prompt Engineering

User interfaces for the most commonly available LLMs allow users to write natural language prompts that effortlessly produce output. Unlike database systems that can require users to input complex query language, LLMs reduce the complexity of the interaction, creating a very user-friendly experience. When LLMs are integrated into other systems like web search engines, the search engine query doubles as a prompt – no special formulations are required. In the end, though, better prompts do yield better output. With that, the field of *prompt engineering* has emerged, encouraging users to help guide the LLM by giving it specific enough instructions for it to be able to carry out the user's desired task.[37]

OpenAI's ChatGPT

ChatGPT was released publicly in November 2022 and quickly became the fastest-growing computer application in history.[38] The Generative Pre-trained Transformer (GPT, of ChatGPT), was originally released by OpenAI in 2018,[39] and work to improve the system has been iterative. OpenAI's GPT-2 came out in 2019; it was larger "with the ability to generate entire articles and perform various language tasks such as translation and summarisation."[40] GPT-2 also served other functions, such as a text-based game engine for the customizable adventures of players of *AI Dungeon 2*.[41] The GPT-3 version was developed by OpenAI and introduced in 2021; "It is specifically designed to generate human-like text in a conversational style"[42] but was also trained on scholarly content, meaning it performs well for writing about research.[43]

At the time it was first released, ChatGPT was using GPT-3, but newer versions of the GPT are now available. In addition, OpenAI is allowing for custom GPTs to be created and used through the ChatGPT interface, making for an increasingly large family of systems. OpenAI's ChatGPT is not the only LLM using a transformer model that is both easy to use and conversational; it is, however, the one that caused a sensation with its release, leaving the competition scrambling to catch up despite some much stronger head starts.

ChatGPT has represented a cultural shift in understanding the promise and affordances of AI, especially for users who otherwise are passive recipients of AI (e.g., when credit card fraud is suspected and their bank alerts them), versus the seemingly new era of access to LLMs that has been ushered in with ChatGPT. In leading the way, ChatGPT has also invited polemics, as the concerns that relate to the use of LLMs have surfaced in discussions of its affordances, but also its drawbacks.

Considerations for Generative AI in Scholarship

Although the considerations mentioned in this section affect uses of GenAI outside of scholarship, a nuanced examination in this context is particularly instructive and serves as a point of departure for the sections of the book that follow. Two kinds of biases that are generally considered in LLMs stem from 1) the training data and 2) the AI algorithm, including the black box that was discussed in the first chapter.[44]

Training Data

LLMs are trained on massive amounts of textual data from sources across the internet. The nature of the underlying data can certainly influence the output that is produced. To arrive at the required volume of content, sources ranging from Wikipedia to Reddit communities have been used, including open-access books and journals. Copyright-protected materials, it seems, have also found their way into the training data of a number of LLMs.

Relying on internet data can be a bit of a double-edged sword. The internet is vast, and the huge number of users and their interests allow for representation by very marginalized and otherwise specialized groups, including linguistically. However, the content that is freely available on the internet is fundamentally limited, with firewalled or analog content not accessible and therefore not included in training data. This excluded content is potentially scholarly. Further, certain voices are amplified online more than others. The memorable experience of Microsoft's Tay chatbot, an AI learning system (LS) that was made available for public interactions through Twitter on March 23, 2016, serves as an example of how content from internet users can be problematic. In less than 24 hours, the chatbot was taken offline for spewing content that was racist, sexist, and antisemitic[45] – content it learned from Twitter users as part of its training. Tay's cautionary tale is an extreme example, but it exemplifies the ways in which the corpus from which systems draw is important. In cases when the training data is bad, the results cannot be expected to rise above.

User Privacy

Privacy has been another concern that LLMs have seen raised – both for personal information contained in their training data and for the information supplied by end-users of LLMs. Outside of the EU, certain versions of

Grammarly, software that uses AI to help with both editing and copyediting, are collecting screen data from users, potentially infringing their right to privacy. When Grammarly users are working with protected data for research participants such as health information or personally identifiable information (PII), the privacy and security of those individuals' data is also at risk.[46] Freely available LLMs tend to allow users to erase their data or opt not to have it collected, but this does put the onus on the user to adjust default settings. Not everyone agrees that GenAI vendors can be trusted to do the right thing with personal data, given their less-than-sterling track record with other protected data such as copyright-protected images and texts.[47]

Concerns have also been raised across the board about the way that LLMs have amassed their training data, citing practices that are fundamentally disrespectful of the individuals whose data is included in their models and a general reticence to confirm inclusion, or, when relating to famous authors like George R. R. Martin, to permit an opt-out.

Hallucinations

LLMs have captured the imaginations of many, including those outside of the scholarly communication ecosystem. Evidence of this includes Dictionary.com's 2023 word of the year: "hallucinate." In this case, *hallucinations* are a reference to the way that LLMs function, with the verb meaning "to produce false information contrary to the intent of the user and present it as if true and factual."[48]

LLMs are designed to pull from the training data on which they were trained but are programmed to provide a few words in a row from any one source. To flesh out an entire sentence requires merging content from any number of sources in order to arrive at acceptable output. Separately, each source might (or might not) be accurate. Merged together, the chances for accuracy diminish. Reinforcement learning ensures that output is conversational and not offensive but does not audit for accuracy. In other words, LLMs are designed to produce strikingly well-written prose, even if the words strung together do not make logic sense. Put another way, LLMs are not meant to be question-answering systems, even if they produce authoritative-sounding text.

Believability of LLM Outputs

The problem of the anthropomorphized intelligence of AI is associated with believable LLM outputs. After all, the uncanny way that LLMs confidently and authoritatively present their output invites believability. Who can quarrel, after all, with assertive statements that are so credibly presented?

Eva A. M. van Dis and colleagues assert that the ability for LLM-generated texts to sound so convincing is associated with the *halo effect*, the tendency to let oneself be convinced of something as a result of a good impression. Unrelated initially to AI, the halo effect was first identified at least 100 years ago by Edward L. Thorndike.[49] Thorndike describes "judgments of the qualities" of a person that reflects the perception of the person. For Thorndike, a positive perception of a person yields a positive assessment, such as believing one's colleagues are good scholars because they present as good human beings.[50] In the same way, the elegant content that is produced by LLMs can seem at first blush to be factual, even when utter nonsense. The 2023 interest in hallucinations might be most closely associated with the problem of how unsuspecting many users were.

In terms of technology, the halo effect relates to what is often termed *automation bias*. Automation bias is an overreliance on technology.[51] In unquestioningly using the results of technology, users have the potential to accept errors that they otherwise would not. How many diners in a restaurant, after all, will examine closely a printed bill itemizing their order? The input was still done by a human actor, and human actors are most definitely not infallible.

Embedding Biases

Biases are a problem with the output of LLMs as well. Even if the Twitter bot example given in the beginning of this section is a bit extreme, it serves as a reminder of the kinds of biased and flawed language that is pervasive on the internet. LLMs rely heavily on training data published on the internet. If text has underlying racist propos, it stands to reason that text produced by an LLM will have these same underlying concerns, even if the LLM's reinforcement process discouraged it from producing content that is outright racist. Moreover, content that is missing from the web will also be invisible to the systems being trained, for example, "social movements which are poorly documented and which do not receive significant media attention will not be captured at all."[52]

Unsurprisingly, research projects have consistently cited problems with LLM outputs. Abubakar Abid, Maheen Farooqi, and James Zou looked at the problems of anti-Muslim bias in LLMs as early as 2021.[53] Race can also be problematic, as output may be biased, including based on the LLM's understanding of the race of the user! For example, researchers at Yale University discovered that ChatGPT with GPT-3.5 and GPT-4 both provided simplified summaries of radiology reports if the prompt indicated the user was not White or Asian.[54] Finally, timeliness can be a problem. LLMs consider all content in the training data equally, including old, obsolete, and outdated content, and they do not emphasize newer content in their output as a result.[55] This means that output is time-agnostic. Input from 1933 is on par, in these systems, with text from 2025, which might be alright if describing ancient phenomena but is patently less useful if describing medical breakthroughs.

System-side filters have been applied to protect users from what could be racist or otherwise problematic outputs. Not all systems are getting it right, however. Sometimes, the filters do not function properly, as evidenced in the lawsuit filed in December 2024 against Google for its Character.AI "companion chatbot"'s alleged presentation of "hypersexualized content" to a nine-year-old, and it telling a 17-year-old to engage in self-harm, and that children murdering parents can be justified.[56] Another example of filters not working is the use of ChatGPT by Matthew Livelsberger who exploded a vehicle in Las Vegas on new year's day, 2025 – ChatGPT provided information enabling him to plan the attack.[57] Problematic output has also been associated with images. In early 2024, Google Gemini's efforts to promote racial diversity led to prompts for individuals in Nazi uniforms to return images of Black and east Asian individuals. Google shut down the service's use for creating images of people but not before coming under considerable fire.[58]

Guardrails and Jailbreaking

Companies like Google and OpenAI try to ensure that their systems will provide information that is not offensive or otherwise problematic. Getting around these guardrails has become an activity in which both researchers and hackers are engaged, and it has become known as *jailbreaking*.[59] Researchers have shown it is possible to make different iterations of ChatGPT spew racist slurs,[60] and more recently, to give instructions on how to launder money or export weapons to countries that were under sanction.[61] Even Tessa, the US National Eating Disorders Association's eating disorders chatbot mentioned earlier, showed signs of nefarious activity after her weaknesses were revealed, with hackers trying to trick Tessa into providing harmful answers to questions.[62]

System-Side Assumptions About Prompts

To function, LLMs must make assumptions about the nature of the natural language prompts that are input. In lieu of seeking clarifications, however, prompts are interpreted at something akin to face value, without any kind of prompt negotiation process. In other words, although interactions with LLMs seem like genuine interactions, they are not. As Jakob Svensson states, "AI-powered automated systems do not acknowledge not-knowing, and as a consequence are incapable of dealing with the unknown."[63] Despite any anthropomorphized intelligence they seem to possess, because LLMs are not designed to *understand,* the user's question and their desired response are not taken into consideration. Instead, a prompt is input, and a response is given. As to how closely that output reflects the intentionality of the request, that is not actually a consideration.

As an example, Tomer Ullman, a psychologist at Harvard University discovered that

> If a container was described as transparent, the machines would fail to infer that someone could see into it. The machines had difficulty taking into account the testimony of people in these situations, and sometimes couldn't distinguish between an object being inside a container and being on top of it.[64]

Trouble abounds in the way prompts are perceived by LLMs, which may or may not be evident in the nature of the output. The assumptions that humans, in their embodied realities, project onto LLMs are not clarified nor are they taken into account by the systems.

Producing *Slop*

The use of AI can be associated with laziness, sometimes with disastrous results.[65] The output is also often associated with poor quality. One of the words shortlisted for the Oxford Word of the Year 2024 was *slop*, meaning low-quality or inaccurate content generated through the use of GenAI. Oxford University Press saw a 332% increase in the term's usage in 2024, aligning with GenAI-created content being seen as "inferior,"[66] presumably due to concerns like hallucinations and potentially also biased output.

At the same time, humans can already carry out shoddy scholarship without the help of LLMs. Humans are biased, they make mistakes, and sometimes those mistakes are intentional as in the case of research fraud. Concerns about GenAI should be taken seriously, and the scholarly community has an obligation to lead the way in understanding the affordances as well as the drawbacks of these systems and their outputs. At best, they are reflections of what already exists – with the addition of a possible layer of *slop*. Humans certainly can produce slop on their own, but with the advent of LLMs, they are much more readily able to produce it in massive quantities, and at the touch of a button.

As AI continues to improve and as specialized systems emerge to support scholarship, scholars doing a range of work might find themselves able to make use of AI-powered tools and systems in support of their research and writing. The next chapter considers some AI tools that can be of use to scholars across the board, in a number of disciplines and at a variety of points in their careers.

Notes

1 Sheela Kolluri et al., "Machine Learning and Artificial Intelligence in Pharmaceutical Research and Development: A Review," *The AAPS Journal* 24, no. 1 (January 2022): 3–10, https://doi.org/10.1208/s12248-021-00644-3.

2 For example, Kolluri et al., "Machine Learning and Artificial Intelligence in Pharmaceutical Research and Development"; Association of Research Libraries (ARL) and Coalition for Networked Information (CNI), *ARL/CNI AI Scenarios: AI-Influenced Futures* (Washington, DC and West Chester, PA: Association of Research Libraries, Coalition for Networked Information and Stratus Inc., June 2024), https://www.arl.org/wp-content/uploads/2024/05/AI-Scenarios.pdf.

3 Ben Lutkevich, "What Is an Expert System?," *TechTarget*, August 2024, https://www.techtarget.com/searchenterpriseai/definition/expert-system.

4 Kyle Wiggers Stringer Cody Corrall, Alyssa, "ChatGPT: Everything You Need to Know About the AI Chatbot," *TechCrunch* (blog), December 4, 2024, https://techcrunch.com/2024/12/04/chatgpt-everything-to-know-about-the-ai-chatbot/.

5 Michele L. McNeal and David Newyear, "Introducing Chatbots in Libraries," in *Streamlining Information Services Using Chatbots, Library Technology Reports* (American Library Association, November–December 2013), 5–10.

6 Daysia Tolentino, "NEDA Pulls Chatbot after Users Say It Gave Harmful Dieting Tips," *NBC News*, June 1, 2023, https://www.nbcnews.com/tech/neda-pulls-chatbot-eating-advice-rcna87231.

7 Nico Klingler, "The Ultimate Guide to AI Models (2024)," *viso.ai*, December 2, 2023, https://viso.ai/deep-learning/ml-ai-models/.

8 Ellen Chetwynd, "Ethical Use of Artificial Intelligence for Scientific Writing: Current Trends," *Journal of Human Lactation* 40, no. 2 (May 2024): 211, https://doi.org/10.1177/08903344241235160.

9 IBM, "What Is Computer Vision?," July 27, 2021, https://www.ibm.com/topics/computer-vision.

10 Gaudenz Boesch, "Supervised vs Unsupervised Learning for Computer Vision," *viso.ai*, December 21, 2023, https://viso.ai/deep-learning/supervised-vs-unsupervised-learning/.

11 Cade Metz, "Using A.I. to Find Bias in A.I.," *The New York Times, SEC. Technology*, June 30, 2021, https://www.nytimes.com/2021/06/30/technology/artificial-intelligence-bias.html.

12 IBM, "What Is Unsupervised Learning?," September 23, 2021, https://www.ibm.com/topics/unsupervised-learning.

13 IBM, "What Is Unsupervised Learning?"; IBM, "What Is Topic Modeling?," March 25, 2024, https://www.ibm.com/topics/topic-modeling.

14 Martin Paul Eve et al., *Reading Peer Review*, 1st ed. (Cambridge University Press, 2020), 63, https://doi.org/10.1017/9781108783521.

15 Caitlin Doogan, Wray Buntine, and Henry Linger, "A Systematic Review of the Use of Topic Models for Short Text Social Media Analysis," *Artificial Intelligence Review* 56, no. 12 (December 2023): 14223–55, https://doi.org/10.1007/s10462-023-10471-x.

16 Xing Yi and James Allan, "Evaluating Topic Models for Information Retrieval" (Proceedings of the 17th ACM Conference on Information and Knowledge Management, CIKM08: Conference on Information and Knowledge Management, Napa Valley California USA: ACM, 2008), 1431–32, https://doi.org/10.1145/1458082.1458317.

17 Wenyi Shang, Rongqian Ma, and Heather Moulaison-Sandy, "How Does Digital Humanities Research Talk About AI?: A Bibliometric Analysis" (Information Research, iConference 2025, Bloomington, IN, 2025) *Information Research* (iConf 2025) 30 (2025): 635–645, https://doi.org/10.47989/ir30iConf47242.

18 For example, Seema Rani and Mukesh Kumar, "Topic Modeling and Its Applications in Materials Science and Engineering," *Materials Today: Proceedings, Second International Conference on Aspects of Materials Science and Engineering (ICAMSE 2021)* 45 (January 1, 2021): 5591–96, https://doi.org/10.1016/j.matpr.2021.02.313.

19 Klingler, "The Ultimate Guide to AI Models (2024)."

20 IBM, "What Is Deep Learning?," June 17, 2024, https://www.ibm.com/topics/deep-learning.

21 IBM, "What Is a Transformer Model?," October 10, 2023, https://www.ibm.com/topics/transformer-model.

22 IBM, "What Is Deep Learning?"

23 Dani Di Placido, "'Demonic' AI-Generated 'Will Smith Eating Spaghetti' Clip Goes Viral," *Forbes*, April 3, 2023, https://www.forbes.com/sites/danidiplacido/2023/04/03/will-smith-eating-spaghetti-is-the-latest-ai-generated-eldritch-abomination/.

24 The-MatrixAgent, "The Difference That One Year of AI Videos Is Mind-Blowing," *Reddit Post, R/Interestingasfuck*, February 17, 2024, www.reddit.com/r/interestingasfuck/comments/1asoyc4/the_difference_that_one_year_of_ai_videos_is/.

25 "AI Firms Will Soon Exhaust Most of the Internet's Data," *Economist*, July 27, 2024, 59, https://www.economist.com/schools-brief/2024/07/23/ai-firms-will-soon-exhaust-most-of-the-internets-data.

26 Michael Humor, "Understanding 'Tokens' and Tokenization in Large Language Models," *Medium*, February 8, 2024, https://blog.devgenius.io/understanding-tokens-and-tokenization-in-large-language-models-1058cd24b944.

27 "AI Firms Will Soon Exhaust Most of the Internet's Data," 59.

28 IBM, "Tips for Writing Foundation Model Prompts: Prompt Engineering," September 18, 2024, https://www.ibm.com/docs/en/watsonx/saas?topic=models-prompt-tips.

29 Emily M. Bender et al., "On the Dangers of Stochastic Parrots: Can Language Models be Too Big? 🦜" (Proceedings of the 2021 ACM Conference on Fairness, Accountability, and Transparency, FAccT '21: 2021 ACM Conference on Fairness, Accountability, and Transparency, Virtual Event Canada: ACM, 2021), 610, https://doi.org/10.1145/3442188.3445922.

30 IBM, "What Is NLP (Natural Language Processing)?," September 23, 2021, https://www.ibm.com/topics/natural-language-processing.

31 Bender et al., "On the Dangers of Stochastic Parrots."

32 IBM, "What Are Large Language Models (LLMs)?," November 2, 2023, https://www.ibm.com/topics/large-language-models.

33 Adam Pasick, "Artificial Intelligence Glossary: Neural Networks and Other Terms Explained," *The New York Times*, *SEC. Technology*, March 27, 2023, https://www.nytimes.com/article/ai-artificial-intelligence-glossary.html.

34 IBM, "What Is Reinforcement Learning from Human Feedback (RLHF)?," November 10, 2023, https://www.ibm.com/topics/rlhf.

35 Tiffany H. Kung et al., "Performance of ChatGPT on USMLE: Potential for AI-Assisted Medical Education Using Large Language Models," ed. Alon Dagan, *PLoS Digital Health* 2, no. 2 (February 9, 2023): 2, https://doi.org/10.1371/journal.pdig.0000198.

36 Pasick, "Artificial Intelligence Glossary."

37 IBM, "What Is Reinforcement Learning from Human Feedback (RLHF)?"

38 Krystal Hu, "ChatGPT Sets Record for Fastest-Growing User Base – Analyst Note," *Reuters, SEC. Technology*, February 2, 2023, https://www.reuters.com/technology/chatgpt-sets-record-fastest-growing-user-base-analyst-note-2023-02-01/.

39 Matthieu Ollivier et al., "A Deeper Dive into ChatGPT: History, Use and Future Perspectives for Orthopaedic Research," *Knee Surgery, Sports Traumatology, Arthroscopy* 31, no. 4 (April 2023): 1190–92, https://doi.org/10.1007/s00167-023-07372-5.

40 Ollivier et al., "A Deeper Dive into ChatGPT," 1190.

41 Minh Hua and Rita Raley, "Playing with Unicorns: AI Dungeon and Citizen NLP," *Digital Humanities Quarterly* 14, no. 4 (2020), https://www.digitalhumanities.org/dhq/vol/14/4/000533/000533.html.

42 Debby R. E. Cotton, Peter A. Cotton, and J. Reuben Shipway, "Chatting and Cheating: Ensuring Academic Integrity in the Era of ChatGPT," *Innovations in Education and Teaching International* 61, no. 2 (March 3, 2024): 228, https://doi.org/10.1080/14703297.2023.2190148.

43 Ollivier et al., "A Deeper Dive into ChatGPT."

44 IBM, "What Is AI Bias?," December 14, 2023, https://www.ibm.com/topics/ai-bias.

45 Gina Neff and Peter Nagy, "Talking to Bots: Symbiotic Agency and the Case of Tay," *International Journal of Communication* 10 (2016): 4915–31; M. J. Wolf, K. Miller, and F. S. Grodzinsky, "Why We Should Have Seen That Coming," *ACM SIGCAS Computers and Society* 47, no. 3 (2017): 54–64.

46 See, for example, the University of Missouri's rationale for only allowing faculty to use the enterprise Grammarly for Education version of the software package: "Grammarly for Education | University of Missouri System," accessed December 13, 2024, https://www.umsystem.edu/ums/is/infosec/grammarly-education.

47 "A Matter of Trust," *Nature* 449, no. 7163 (October 2007): 637–38, https://doi.org/10.1038/449637b.

48 Nick Norlen and Grant Barrett, "Word of the Year 2023," accessed December 5, 2024, https://content.dictionary.com/word-of-the-year-2023/.

49 Eva A. M. van Dis et al., "ChatGPT: Five Priorities for Research," *Nature* 614, no. 7947 (February 9, 2023): 224–26, https://doi.org/10.1038/d41586-023-00288-7.

50 Edward L. Thorndike, "A Constant Error in Psychological Ratings," *Journal of Applied Psychology* 4, no. 1 (1920): 25, https://doi.org/10.1037/h0071663.

51 Kate Goddard, Abdul Roudsari, and Jeremy C. Wyatt, "Automation Bias: A Systematic Review of Frequency, Effect Mediators, and Mitigators," *Journal of the American Medical Informatics Association* 19, no. 1 (January 2012): 121–27, https://doi.org/10.1136/amiajnl-2011-000089.

52 Bender et al., "On the Dangers of Stochastic Parrots," 614.
53 Abubakar Abid, Maheen Farooqi, and James Zou, "Persistent Anti-Muslim Bias in Large Language Models," in *Proceedings of the 2021 AAAI/ACM Conference on AI, Ethics, and Society, AIES '21* (New York, NY, USA: Association for Computing Machinery, 2021), 298–306, https://doi.org/10.1145/3461702.3462624.
54 Kanhai S. Amin, Howard P. Forman, and Melissa A. Davis, "Even with ChatGPT, Race Matters," *Clinical Imaging* 109 (May 2024): 110113, https://doi.org/10.1016/j.clinimag.2024.110113.
55 Chetwynd, "Ethical Use of Artificial Intelligence for Scientific Writing," 213.
56 Bobby Allyn, "Lawsuit: A Chatbot Hinted a Kid Should Kill His Parents over Screen Time Limits," *NPR, SEC. Business*, December 10, 2024, https://www.npr.org/2024/12/10/nx-s1-5222574/kids-character-ai-lawsuit; Clare Duffy, "Character.AI Allegedly Told an Autistic Teen It Was OK to Kill His Parents. They're Suing to Take Down the App | CNN Business," *CNN*, December 10, 2024, https://www.cnn.com/2024/12/10/tech/character-ai-second-youth-safety-lawsuit/index.html.
57 Emma Tucker, "Green Beret Who Exploded Cybertruck in Las Vegas Used AI to Plan Blast," *CNN*, January 7, 2025, https://www.cnn.com/2025/01/07/us/las-vegas-cybertruck-explosion-livelsberger/index.html.
58 Andrew Fenton, "Google to Fix Diversity-Borked Gemini AI, ChatGPT Goes Insane: AI Eye," *Cointelegraph Magazine* (blog), February 22, 2024, https://cointelegraph.com/magazine/google-fix-diversity-borked-gemini-chatgpt-goes-insane-ai-eye/.
59 Matt Burgess, "The Hacking of ChatGPT Is Just Getting Started," *Wired*, April 13, 2023, https://www.wired.com/story/chatgpt-jailbreak-generative-ai-hacking/.
60 Dhiraj Murthy, "Using Web Science to Improve Platform Accountability" (15th ACM Web Science Conference 2023, Austin, Texas, May 1, 2023), https://www.youtube.com/watch?v=esdtIWoXfWI.
61 Anna Cooban, "ChatGPT Can be Tricked into Telling People How to Commit Crimes, a Tech Firm Finds | CNN Business," *CNN*, October 23, 2024, https://www.cnn.com/2024/10/23/business/chatgpt-tricked-commit-crimes/index.html.
62 Tolentino, "NEDA Pulls Chatbot After Users Say It Gave Harmful Dieting Tips."
63 Jakob Svensson, "Artificial Intelligence Is an Oxymoron: The Importance of an Organic Body When Facing Unknown Situations as They Unfold in the Present Moment," *AI & Society* 38, no. 1 (February 2023): 367, https://doi.org/10.1007/s00146-021-01311-z.
64 Oliver Whang, "Can a Machine Know That We Know What It Knows?," *The New York Times, SEC. Science*, March 27, 2023, https://www.nytimes.com/2023/03/27/science/ai-machine-learning-chatbots.html.
65 Douglas MacMillan, David Ovalle, and Aaron Schaffer, "Arrested by AI: Police Ignore Standards after Facial Recognition Matches," *The Washington Post (Online), SEC. Business*, January 13, 2025, https://www.proquest.com/docview/3154984885/citation/DAA20F789EF64A71PQ/1.
66 *Oxford Word of the Year 2024* (Oxford University Press, 2024), https://corp.oup.com/word-of-the-year/.

4 AI's Potential for Use in Scholarship

The work of scholars is being shaped and reshaped at scale by AI technologies. Both research and writing have benefited from technological advances supported by natural language processing (NLP), machine learning (ML), and most recently, generative AI (GenAI) systems, but so have other aspects of the work. Jennifer Chubb and colleagues have conceptualized the way that AI can be used in the research process as being either 1) able to support collective research endeavors (e.g., the advancement of a field or an institution) or 2) able to support the research and writing practices of an individual, and through their publications, supporting the larger collectivity.[1] Through surveys of faculty in a range of disciplines, they affirm that the bulk of the uses of AI in the academy are currently for individual benefit, and to support mundane tasks, while increasing productivity. Drawing from these same kinds of influences, this chapter primarily looks at ways that AI is having and will have implications for authors as part of the scholarly communication process.

With the rise of chatbots and increasing advances in AI, expectations and practices surrounding the tools available and the way research is created and consumed will change accordingly. Implications for authors are manyfold, as they adapt to revised approaches to research, writing, and consuming content. All told, AI is providing support that is specialized and niche but also readily available through generative systems. For many of the AI-powered approaches described here, the technologies and their results are imperfect but are improving constantly.

Idea Generation

One strength of GenAI systems is the ability to help with brainstorming. Indeed, this is one way experts[2] are encouraging university-level writing instructors to use GenAI in their classes. Systems like ChatGPT can help with brainstorming, relying on their massive training data for a variety of perspectives.[3] Even then, though, van Dis and colleagues issue the warning that "[r]esearchers who use ChatGPT risk being misled by false or biased information,"[4] and they could subsequently be fooled into working from a faulty

DOI: 10.4324/9781003570325-4

point of departure. As long as users are cautious, and unwilling to blindly accept suggestions without reflection, the partnership may well be sound. For example, experts in pedagogy describe how large language models (LLMs) can support idea generation for research and analysis[5] and can "hint . . . at unexplored aspects and current research topics."[6] All told, the judicious use of LLMs for brainstorming is one way of conceptualizing GenAI's contribution to scholarship.[7]

Research Support

As previously explored, AI can take on somewhat mundane research support roles, allowing scholars to focus on the more specialized aspects of the work that require human intelligence. One case in point is how AI is helping lab-based science with some very practical aspects of the work. AI can manage lab equipment, scheduling maintenance and purchasing the needed supplies.[8] But increasingly, AI can also help with the many specialized roles associated with research, including aspects of work with reviewing the extant literature and with management of the project's data.

Identifying Relevant Sources

Standard scholarly communication practices and norms of science require scholars to create new knowledge. This is done by establishing what has been done and situating in that body of literature. A thorough understanding of the extant literature informs the work of scholars, therefore, as their reviews of a field's literature

> often lead to ideas for new studies because they help to identify research problems and gaps and justify the relevance and timeliness of addressing them. They serve as foundations and frameworks for research projects because they help to develop an understanding of a domain and explain the topic under study. Moreover, because they guide data collection and analysis, they also inform theory development and testing. Done correctly, they can significantly improve the outcome of research projects.[9]

AI-powered systems, including LLMs, can help with many aspects of work relating to the analysis of the body of work in a given field.

Online indexes and databases allow for quick access to references and, often, to the articles themselves. Standard approaches in the sciences and social sciences require a scholar (or their assistant) to read through these articles, selecting the most relevant and using them as a basis for designing the study to be carried out and as a way against which to consider the findings. This task, however, has become increasingly unrealistic with the proliferation of venues and the rapid increase in the number of articles.[10]

AI-powered systems are changing this paradigm and supporting the need to identify the most relevant and important works, and to help make sense of them. For scholars interested in quickly arriving at a place from which they can springboard directly into their research, AI can help. These systems, many of which are available at little or no cost, combine features at which AI excels – finding sources from within a huge corpus of content and ensuring that the most relevant content is identified can greatly simplify the process.

AI-Powered Search Engines

Search engines that make use of AI specifically are marketed to support scholars in their efforts to identify and access relevant scholarly literature. Although the ubiquitous web search engines that have been around for years are now using AI to enhance their results, specialized search engines that focus on providing access to scholarly articles are able to help researchers identify the most relevant scholarly sources.

Standalone scholarly article search engine systems exist that provide results based on an assembled corpus of scholarly articles derived notably from open-access sources. Other AI search engines are querying databases of articles assembled by publishers and vendors seeking to draw value from their collections in a time when those collections are increasingly available online for free through both legitimate means (e.g., open access agreements) and unscrupulous ones (e.g., SciHub, a service that provides unauthorized access to copyright-protected scholarly articles). Scopus AI[11] is one example of a vendor's AI-powered search engine. Some AI-powered search engines exist that also support enhanced search and discovery, with some supporting discovery and allowing researchers to compile notes.

Personalized Recommendations

Recommender systems were first introduced in 1995[12] and have evolved since, primarily as a way to support the personalized discovery of resources (e.g., Netflix films) or items (e.g., products on Amazon). "The aim of the recommender system is to lower the user's search effort by listing those items of highest utility."[13] In other words, recommender systems predict resources that will be relevant, given the specifics of the user and their domain; in the case of scholars seeking articles, such systems are valuable for saving the time of scholars but also for helping ensure a thorough sweep of available literature.

In scholarly environments, understanding basic information about a scholar (i.e., "knowledge-based recommendations") allows for meaningful "more like this" recommendations for a searcher whose profile is known.

A knowledge of what other, similar searchers have appreciated (i.e., "collaborative filtering-based") can also help inform the recommendations, as can an understanding of the content of the article selected (i.e., "content-based recommendations").[14] Combined, these aspects of AI-powered search allow for better, more personalized results that are more relevant and more quickly identified than a searcher would have done on their own.

Culling Through Sources

Once sources are identified, AI-powered systems, especially LLMs, can also help with understanding what content is relevant and how it relates to the work at hand. This help can come in a number of related ways, including working directly with individual articles, as well as overviews of sets of articles. AI can help with making sense of individual sources, making connections between papers, and synthesizing their main ideas. Because systems may blend together a number of these features, it is helpful to examine each feature separately.

Summarizing and Synthesizing Sources

Recent advances in AI have paved the way for better automation of language-based tasks, including the creation of summaries of works. Taking into consideration the text of the article (which should include the abstract, keywords, author affiliations, and other information), another class of AI-powered tools is designed to help with the summarization and analysis of articles. Summaries can support the quick consumption of content. Further, specific aspects of an article might be important to understand, and some systems allow users to isolate information about the methodology or research design, including sample size and other information relevant to understanding how best to conduct a study. Multiple texts can also be synthesized at once, creating a high-level summary that allows for comparisons. As with every other AI-powered technology described here, the results will need to be confirmed, but overviews of articles created by AI nonetheless provide potential insight that might otherwise have been missed by human readers.

Other strategies for using summarization services include the creation of full-length summaries of a piece – in other words, restating text that for some reason might need to be finessed. Article-length summaries can smooth grammatical and linguistic anomalies, which can be helpful for non-native speakers of a language or for authors who would like feedback on structuring their own prose. Conversely, these systems might also help avoid plagiarism detection when used by bad actors intentionally reusing an existing source and wishing to present it as their own new work.

Chatting With Sources

A number of AI-powered systems propose that researchers "chat" with the full text of documents to ask specific questions. Just as ChatGPT is a chatbot that allows prompts to be entered that ask questions, so too are the chatbots that allow researchers to ask questions about a research article or document such as legislation. Chatting allows researchers to quickly and easily engage with the source in a way that goes beyond a simple summary. For example, users might ask about top three findings presented in an article and their importance, but to have the output provided in another language. Specifics about the work in question, comparisons to other articles, recommendations about related pieces, and other bespoke feedback can be solicited. Among other things, the ability to chat with sources presents a way for novice researchers to begin to engage with primary source documents.

Depending on the system, some article chatbots might permit multi-article interactions where a researcher chats with more than one article at a time to assess the similarities and differences. This might help with the identification of trends in the papers. It might also help in the detection of research gaps. Finally, the detection of findings that contradict each other or that can be more richly understood in a broader context can also take place.

Conceptualizing and Visualizing Connections

AI can also support an understanding of the relationships between articles, helping researchers conceptualize how papers are similar or different. These specialized systems enable researchers to visualize connections between articles, in the process potentially discovering new or unexpected connections in the published literature.[15] By seeing how articles relate to each other and to the questions being asked, researchers are better able to situate their own work, to understand how their methodologies and approaches relate to previous work, to understand how their results relate to prior results, and in the process, to craft more compelling discussions of their work and how it is situated in the broader research context.

AI-powered systems have emerged that use visualization techniques to show authors the connections between research articles. These connections can be based on shared references. When articles share references, they can be assumed to share intellectual similarities and reasonably, to be on the same or at least an adjacent topic. Articles might also share other similarities that AI can identify, including disciplinary or methodological. At the same time, sussing out 1) the aboutness of articles and 2) characteristics of articles allows for different articles to be brought together. In this way, AI-powered systems can make explicit the connections that are otherwise implicit in recommender systems (e.g., "content-based recommendations"), creating new products in the process. Scholars, especially ones new to a field, can benefit a good deal from the former, where connections between articles in a field are explicit. Seasoned researchers, on the other hand, might be seen to benefit more from the latter approach, when they have already internalized the basic connections in the field, and through the use of AI-powered systems are able to expand their understanding of a phenomenon or approach based on work done in other areas.

Formulating the Literature Review

An important part of the scholarly communication process involves situating one's work in the body of work in a field. In formal scholarly writing, not only for researchers wishing to publish but also for novice scholars learning to write, identifying relevant research and presenting how it pertains to the work at hand is an important step in formulating one's own research and situating it. In the sciences and the social sciences, reviews of the literature are an essential part of the scholarly article and in formal venues like theses and dissertations. Literature reviews can also be articles in their own right (e.g., "review papers," systematic reviews, and meta-analyses). There is an art to crafting the literature review, and among other things it should be structured conceptually rather than presenting as a list.[16] AI can help with all of this.

Automated Literature Reviews

AI can help with creating standard reviews of the literature, especially as they are used in the sciences and social sciences. Specially created systems are emerging that support both the identification of relevant literature and its writeup for use in scholarly venues. At the time of writing, the systems on the market that purport to simplify this task for researchers are still in their infancy, but given the availability of systems that independently find, organize, connect, and synthesize research, the ability for researchers to craft their own review of the literature is well supported with AI-powered systems, even if these systems are imperfect.[17]

Work With Data

Although benefits for researchers of working directly with their data might exist, there are certainly advantages to shortcutting some of the efforts that can go into the process while gaining a technology-enhanced perspective on the big picture. AI-powered systems can promote efficiency and accuracy, while doing better work, faster, and with deeper insights, and can help with data processing and analysis.

Data Collection and Cleaning

AI-powered systems can help with data collection and analysis. Depending on the kind of work being done and the legal limitations involved, AI-driven systems can scrape data from the web and retain it for analysis. Speech recognition systems using AI can facilitate the transcription of interview data, for example, allowing for the analysis of the text of the interview to follow. AI-powered systems can also allow for data collection from monitoring devices. For example, drones and satellites can capture data in ecological systems. Similarly, sensors can be used to collect measurements – both outside (e.g., temperatures) and in lab-based environments. Sensors in labs present exciting opportunities for research in these environments, where machines can oversee the work once it is underway.

AI can also help with aspects of work with data, including preprocessing and cleaning, outlier detection, and data imputation. The problem of biased datasets can likewise begin to be addressed with AI, since

> bias can creep into a system when designers choose the wrong data or sort through it in the wrong way. Studies show that face-recognition services can be biased against women and people of color when they are trained on photo collections dominated by white men.[18]

Although not perfect, as with other tools and systems described here, applying one of the available AI tools to a dataset can represent one step to helping ensure quality and equity.

Data Analysis

Depending on the field and the methodology, analyzing data can be an essential part of the research process. Diminishing time spent on such tasks, however, has the potential to enable a broader reach for research through the analysis of larger datasets. An analysis of larger datasets has the potential to increase insights. Further, computers can identify patterns in large datasets more readily than humans, which suggests the possibility of a closer analysis of the data being investigated.

Although not perfect, AI can help with labor-intensive work such as pattern recognition in image, video, and text. An example in the biological sciences is where researchers have set up video recorders in remote areas to capture movement patterns of specific animals, which are then analyzed by AI. AI can help with sorting through the data to identify the movements of the tigers in question, ignoring the other beasts roaming the habitat. Qualitative data analysis, including text-based analysis like the content of textual data (documents, interviews, etc.) and the axial coding of qualitative survey data has also been facilitated by AI-powered systems. Many qualitative data analysis software packages are free to download and use, and in the case of Leximancer, the software package has been used by researchers since the mid-2000s.[19] Depending on the software and the extensiveness of the use of

AI, these packages can cluster and classify text (and video) based on similarities and code it accordingly. They can find and identify frequently mentioned words or phrases. All told, these software packages can be used in support of common qualitative methodologies such as sentiment analysis, discourse analysis, and thematic analysis.

Allowing for analyses that would be painstakingly long to carry out, if not impossible, AI-powered systems nonetheless do their analyses quickly and efficiently. The anthropomorphized intelligence can be quite convincing, though, and as black boxes, the systems are not infallible. They do represent, however, trusted tools that are increasingly in use. As with some of the other AI-powered systems supporting research and writing, they allow for the scalability of work, enabling a single researcher or a modest team to carry out expansive analyses.

Writing Support

Much as a broad range of scholars can benefit from AI's help with research, scholars of all levels can benefit from help with writing. And like many of the systems for research that are based on LLMs and are either free or low-cost, writing support (especially in the form of LLMs) can be easy to access for many scholars. The benefits are immediate. LLMs generate text that is beautifully error-free in terms of grammatical and typographical elements, highlighting the anthropomorphized intelligence behind the work. At the same time, however, the content might be deeply flawed, including inaccuracies resulting from the way the systems are encoded, weak argumentations, or circular logic.[20]

Accordingly, only human actors are able to participate fully in the authoring process. This does not mean, however, that no context exists in which a human actor might use an AI for help with writing; in fact, writing support is regularly integrated in the tools most authors use. Even using LLMs might be appropriate in a limited capacity, depending on the context. In specific cases where the use of LLMs is allowed, style guides such as the one by the American Psychological Association (APA) have endorsed citing ChatGPT and other generative AI software as a source, and providing both the prompt and the text produced, as well as describing any other uses (such as for reviewing the literature) in the methodology or introduction.[21] In this way, the agency of the author is well understood, as is the way the text returned by the software was critiqued, edited, and adapted for use by the author.

Copyediting

Human actors have been involved in copyediting and in guiding the final outcome of writing by suggesting changes, additions, and modifications to an author's text. Editing and copyediting can be done professionally, by a copy editor or other editor (book editor, column editor, or others); formally by a dissertation advisor or committee member or writing center peer support; or informally by a friend, relative, or classmate. AI-powered copyediting systems mirror the systems that have developed around human actors. A number of these have been around since the early 2000s if not longer and some of the most reliable and well-honed are the grammar and typographical error checkers integrated into word processing software like Microsoft Word and Google Docs. Although these systems are not infallible due to their incomplete dictionaries and inability to evaluate a term's correctness based on the context, for most writing, they are incredibly helpful. In the scholarly communication process, presenting grammatical work that is free of typographical errors is held in high regard, with content not meeting these standards often disparaged regardless of the quality of the ideas.

Autocomplete and Auto-Suggest

Natural language processing systems allow word processing software to help facilitate the writing process by suggesting either the letters needed to complete a word, or the words needed to complete a phrase or sentence. The former, *autocomplete*, allows for a word-by-word advancement, whereas *auto-suggest* suggests whole words or phrases. Using the corpus of documents having been written on their software as a point of departure, systems are able to present possible content to authors without much effort. Each of these two options, autocomplete and auto-suggest, has the potential to radically change the content that finds its way onto the page. Specifically, since scholarly writing is so specialized, and since the corpus from which autocomplete and auto-suggest draw is not necessarily scholarly, the potential for the tone or voice to be misaligned with the scholarly purpose is undeniable. Further, the content itself is also likely to be misaligned with the topic and purpose of the work, leading the scholarly author to repeatedly type through suggestions that are not helpful. Imperfect, as the other AI-powered products described here, autocomplete and autosuggest can facilitate the writing task but will need to be carefully overseen.

Editing

The idea generation and brainstorming function mentioned in the beginning of this chapter can extend to approaches to structuring an essay. LLMs can help generate the potential structure to an essay, much the way a writing coach or editor could help. Although as Franziska Tsufim and Lainie Pomerleau[22] clarify, these systems are not able to suggest lines of argumentation. Instead, they are able to restructure. One successful commercial product that supports automated changes to essay structures is Grammarly.[23] Systems like these help revise text in the way a professional copyeditor or developmental editor might, suggesting different placement for text, adjustments to tone or voice, and other kinds of changes that do not fundamentally change the ideas present but that streamline them, enhance them, or rearrange them for enhanced consumption by readers.

Writers can also use LLMs to craft lists of topics to cover or outlines for the projects they have conceptualized. They can brainstorm titles or workshop elements of an abstract; they can ask for ideas about venues for publication. A boon to human creativity, LLMs are good sources of ideas that have already been put forth, in some capacity.

Specialized Support for Writing

Although adequate for idea generation and smoothing writing with proper oversight, general-purpose generative AI is not yet a reliable source for scholarly writing. AI-powered systems have been developed that are designed to help scholars and that will not, for example, hallucinate references in the same way that ChatGPT will.[24] One of the ways researchers can create resources personalized to their research interests is through the creation of their own bespoke GPT, or the use of one via OpenAI's ChatGPT interface that has been created either by ChatGPT or by a third party. A number of the GPTs currently available through OpenAI's interface are designed to help with scholarship, including GPTs that offer to help with summarizing recent research, writing the introduction to an article and including references, and those that "humanize" text written by an LLM.

These systems show promise. As with the other LLMs, however, they produce work that is not always accurate, that does not reason, and that must be carefully checked even when revising text for readability (and not for content generation) in order to be used.

Machine Translation

Machine translation is another field that has been around since at least the year 2000. AI-powered translation became prominent with the advent of Google Translate in 2012 – a system that harvested the web and also high-quality digital sources such as scans of books to serve as the training data. The change in approach that AI wrought was stark, and increasingly, the next generation of AI-powered translators continue to be free, performant, and incredibly accurate. Although these systems might be adept at scholarly writing styles, they still can lack the specific vocabulary of a discipline or field. Especially when translating into a scholar's native tongue or to a language in which the author is highly competent, such inaccuracies will be more readily anticipated and managed.

The current generation of free, online AI-powered translators can benefit scholars in a number of ways. First, they can serve to translate existing content (e.g., seminal articles) into a language with which authors are more familiar. For example, if the work is available digitally, a paper that was written in Arabic can be translated into French for consumption by a francophone researcher. Shorter versions of articles can also be produced – summaries instead of translations that capture the full extent of the original.

In addition, these AI-powered translation systems can translate the content that scholars have produced, rendering them in other languages. For example, work in one language can be translated into a lingua franca of scholarship for eventual distribution or publication. In this scenario, a new work written in Spanish might be translated into English for possible publication in an English-language journal. Another reason for translating content is to create abstracts in multiple languages. In this scenario, a conference might create abstracts for proceedings in additional languages or a bilingual or multilingual organization might address the needs of speakers of other languages through automated means.

Scholarly communication is broader than just formal publishing, though, and AI-powered translators offer serious potential for scholars to engage either directly with other scholars or more broadly through social media. Scholars wishing to correspond with others who do not speak their language can use free translators or LLMs to help establish emails that convey the ideas they wish to present and that use the correct tone, a problem that is consistently observed when communicating in a language by non-native speakers. Translators help with consuming digital content as well, from email responses to current awareness searches of social media platforms for information from trusted scholars working in another language. In other words, the power of translation does not have to be felt uniquely in formal publishing venues – with the potential for very meaningful exchanges between scholars and groups of scholars to be facilitated.

Leveling the Playing Field . . .

The potential of AI systems for research and writing is drawing a lot of attention. Many of these systems are incredibly easy to use, making them widely accessible to scholars of all levels and skill sets. Further, many are available for free or at a low cost. Such technologies will likely be able to support the production and consumption of scholarship for low-resourced scholars (e.g., scholars in under-funded disciplines, institutions, geographical locations) as long as they have access to a computer and the internet. In the process of the discovery and use of AI for scholarship, a more level playing field is imagined.[25]

AI-powered systems can be envisioned to help novice scholars explore and embrace a new area of study, in the process allowing them to identify important and pressing questions and to access scholarship that supports their investigation. Academia has adopted an apprenticeship model, which at first will limit junior scholars to the expertise of their supervisors. AI has the potential, in these cases, to allow students to extend beyond the intellectual limitations of those immediately around them, giving them access to the broader body of knowledge in a way that is accessible to them at a beginner level.

Given that mundane work formerly in the purview of human actors is increasingly available to be carried out through AI-powered systems, another hope is that AI will democratize the research and writing process. Where well-resourced institutions engage human actors, under-resourced ones can instead turn to free versions of LLMs. Individuals can take advantage of all sorts of engagement with these systems, from idea generation to research support and beyond. Writing support is a particularly compelling way that LLMs can be used to ensure help for a range of scholars. The ripple effect of having a more level playing field presents the opportunity for scholars who previously would have been denied a voice to produce work that is both important and relevant, thereby benefitting the whole of the scholarly record. In many ways, LLMs present cause for optimism.

In particular, a leveling of the playing field on a purely linguistic level has been discussed as a possible benefit of the availability of LLMs. In the way that translation is quick and easy with services like ChatGPT, this has the potential to allow authors access to primary sources written in languages in which they are not competent. This also potentially allows them not only to smooth out problems with writing when working in a foreign language, as mentioned earlier, but also to translate their work into other languages for publication. Change can be slow, however, and in 2024, patterns of language use in open-access journal articles that might have indicated a more robust shift were still not visible.[26] In other words, optimism is good, but the specifics still seem to be lacking at present.

. . . *Or Further Disenfranchising Scholars?*

The counterpoint to the optimistic enthusiasm for a more level playing field via LLMs must likewise be considered. The problem of a digital divide and the social justice factors playing into this development of a set of "haves" and "have nots" extends to access to and knowledge of digital technologies – including the AI-powered tools used in scholarly communication. Many AI-powered systems offer limited services for free, then charge modest to more significant fees with increased use. Not only is access to a working computer important but also to the funds to support access – the internet connection, the ability to train in prompt creation, the ability to train in how best to use the content created (i.e., the need to review any content generated) – all mean that these technologies might not be as transparent to use as previously imagined, or as inexpensive.

The use of LLMs requires a fair deal of oversight stemming from a fundamental mistrust of the output including the hallucinations and slop that are part of their use. Care must therefore be taken in their deployment. A cursory examination of freely available AI-powered systems' instructions does not reveal the kinds of *caveat emptor* warnings one might expect. Rather, systems are presented as being accurate and providing authoritative results, thanks to what seems to be anthropomorphized intelligence. How an independent scholar would know to be wary is unclear, and the need for caution is unintuitive.

As the Committee on Publication Ethics (COPE) summarizes from its 2024 forum on plagiarism, "Institutions and supervisors are responsible for training more junior researchers in research ethics and values. However, not all have the resources or programs to do this."[27] If intellectual "heavy lifting" is outsourced to LLMs, how then can the scholarly publishing community make clear the need to fact-check that work at every turn? AI cannot substitute for a human advisor or superior, making the use of outputs fraught. And if the underlying dataset is not linguistically representative of a group, that group risks being left behind.[28] This means that AI might not be able to address all questions equally, leaving gaps for unsuspecting scholars who are relying on these systems.

The scholarly communication process is rich and complex, and as AI continues to be integrated into the daily activities of authors, changes to the way authors produce and consume scholarship will continue to be felt. The next chapter considers some of the drawbacks that accompany the use of AI-powered tools in scholarly communication.

Notes

1 Jennifer Chubb, Peter Cowling, and Darren Reed, "Speeding up to Keep up: Exploring the Use of AI in the Research Process," *AI & Society* 37, no. 4 (December 2022): 1439–57, https://doi.org/10.1007/s00146-021-01259-0.

2 For example, Franziska Tsufim and Lainie Pomerleau, "More Is Less?: Using Generative AI for Idea Generation and Diversification in Early Writing Processes," in *Teaching and Generative AI*, ed. Beth Buyserie and Travis N. Thurston (Utah State University, 2024), https://uen.pressbooks.pub/teachingandgenerativeai/chapter/more-is-less-using-generative-ai-for-idea-generation-and-diversification-in-early-writing-processes/.

3 Yun Dai, Ang Liu, and Cher Ping Lim, "Reconceptualizing ChatGPT and Generative AI as a Student-Driven Innovation in Higher Education," *Procedia CIRP* 119 (2023): 84–90, https://doi.org/10.1016/j.procir.2023.05.002.

4 Eva A. M. van Dis et al., "ChatGPT: Five Priorities for Research," *Nature* 614, no. 7947 (February 9, 2023): 224–25, https://doi.org/10.1038/d41586-023-00288-7.

5 Tareq Rasul et al., "The Role of ChatGPT in Higher Education: Benefits, Challenges, and Future Research Directions," *Journal of Applied Learning & Teaching* 6, no. 1 (May 11, 2023), https://doi.org/10.37074/jalt.2023.6.1.29.

6 Enkelejda Kasneci et al., "ChatGPT for Good? On Opportunities and Challenges of Large Language Models for Education," *Learning and Individual Differences* 103 (April 1, 2023): 2–13, https://doi.org/10.1016/j.lindif.2023.102274.

7 Caradee Y. Wright et al., "The African Journal Partnership Program's Guidance on the Use of AI in Scholarly Publishing," *Ghana Medical Journal* 58, no. 1 (March 25, 2024): 2, https://doi.org/10.4314/gmj.v58i1.1.

8 Rick Halton, "How AI Will Impact the Science Laboratory? Here Are 22 Examples," *Sapio Sciences*, March 31, 2023, https://www.sapiosciences.com/blog/how-ai-will-impact-the-science-laboratory-here-are-22-examples/.

9 Jan vom Brocke et al., "Standing on the Shoulders of Giants: Challenges and Recommendations of Literature Search in Information Systems Research," *Communications of the Association for Information Systems* 37, no. 1 (August 1, 2015): 206, https://doi.org/10.17705/1CAIS.03709.

10 For example, vom Brocke et al., "Standing on the Shoulders of Giants."

11 Scopus, "Scopus AI: Trusted Content. Powered by Responsible AI," *www.elsevier.com*, accessed January 15, 2025, https://www.elsevier.com/products/scopus/scopus-ai.

12 Robin Burke, Alexander Felfernig, and Mehmet H. Göker, "Recommender Systems: An Overview," *AI Magazine* 32, no. 3 (June 5, 2011): 13–18, https://doi.org/10.1609/aimag.v32i3.2361.

13 Burke, Felfernig, and Göker, "Recommender Systems," 13.

14 Burke, Felfernig, and Göker, "Recommender Systems"; Qian Zhang, Jie Lu, and Yaochu Jin, "Artificial Intelligence in Recommender Systems," *Complex & Intelligent Systems* 7, no. 1 (February 1, 2021): 439–57, https://doi.org/10.1007/s40747-020-00212-w.

15 Previously, the notion of "undiscovered public knowledge" (Swanson, Don R., "Undiscovered Public Knowledge," *The Library Quarterly* 56, no. 2 (April 1986): 103–18, https://doi.org/10.1086/601720) was used to describe how connections between topics were obscured due to the problem of scholarship being siloed. Now, bibliometric analysis is one way that LBD takes place (Menasha Thilakaratne, Katrina Falkner, and Thushari Atapattu, "A Systematic Review on Literature-Based Discovery: General Overview, Methodology, & Statistical Analysis," *ACM Computing Surveys* 52, no. 6 (November 30, 2020): 1–34, https://doi.org/10.1145/3365756).

16 Jane Webster and Richard T. Watson, "Analyzing the Past to Prepare for the Future: Writing a Literature Review," *MIS Quarterly* 26, no. 2 (2002): xiii–xxiii.

17 Heather Moulaison-Sandy et al., "AI Literature Review Systems: An Analysis of Performance, Affordances and Outputs for a Complex Topic in the Social Sciences," *Information Research an International Electronic Journal* 30, no. iConf (March 11, 2025): 1244–52, https://doi.org/10.47989/ir30iConf46906.

18 Cade Metz, "Using A.I. to Find Bias in A.I.," *The New York Times, SEC. Technology*, June 30, 2021, https://www.nytimes.com/2021/06/30/technology/artificial-intelligence-bias.html.
19 For example, Andrew E. Smith and Michael S. Humphreys, "Evaluation of Unsupervised Semantic Mapping of Natural Language with Leximancer Concept Mapping," *Behavior Research Methods* 38, no. 2 (May 1, 2006): 262–79, https://doi.org/10.3758/BF03192778.
20 For example, the informal analysis of Dirk Lindebaum and Peter Fleming, "ChatGPT Undermines Human Reflexivity, Scientific Responsibility and Responsible Management Research," *British Journal of Management* 35, no. 2 (2024): 566–75, https://doi.org/10.1111/1467-8551.12781.
21 Timothy McAdoo, "How to Cite ChatGPT," *APA Style* (blog), February 23, 2024, https://apastyle.apa.org/blog/how-to-cite-chatgpt; Heather Moulaison-Sandy, "What Is a Person? Emerging Interpretations of AI Authorship and Attribution," *Proceedings of the Association for Information Science and Technology* 60, no. 1 (October 2023): 279–90, https://doi.org/10.1002/pra2.788.
22 Tsufim and Pomerleau, "More Is Less?"
23 "Grammarly: Free AI Writing Assistance," accessed January 14, 2025, https://www.grammarly.com/.
24 For example, Joseph Mugaanyi et al., "Evaluation of Large Language Model Performance and Reliability for Citations and References in Scholarly Writing: Cross-Disciplinary Study," *Journal of Medical Internet Research* 26 (April 5, 2024): e52935, https://doi.org/10.2196/52935.
25 Wright et al., "The African Journal Partnership Program's Guidance on the Use of AI in Scholarly Publishing," 2.
26 Heather Moulaison-Sandy and Amanda Shelton, "Has OA Moved Past a Lingua Franca?," *Proceedings of the Association for Information Science and Technology* 61, no. 1 (October 2024): 604–9, https://doi.org/10.1002/pra2.1066.
27 COPE: Committee on Publication Ethics, "Plagiarism in 2024," *COPE: Committee on Publication Ethics, pt. "Comments"; Bullet 10*, 2024, https://publicationethics.org/resources/forum-discussion-topics/plagiarism-2024.
28 Ellen Chetwynd, "Ethical Use of Artificial Intelligence for Scientific Writing: Current Trends," *Journal of Human Lactation* 40, no. 2 (May 2024): 212, https://doi.org/10.1177/08903344241235160.

5 Implications for the Scholarly Record

The way that scholarship is carried out has been changing over time.[1] The technologies, including AI technologies, that have impacted scholarship and writing since at least 2000 are continuing to shift practice. The scholarly record will have no choice but to reflect these changes. AI can have many positive impacts on the research process and the writing and publishing process. One perceived benefit is the ability of scholars to work together more easily and in the process, allowing them to engage in more impactful "blue skies" research as well as to draw benefit from interdisciplinary perspectives.[2] The creation of new knowledge is facilitated by new uses of technology, and the scholarly record bears witness to and benefits from these changes.

AI's support of scholarship has enhanced progress and facilitated advances. At the same time, the metaphors mentioned in the first chapter influence the ways that AI can contribute to research and to the scholarly record. The anthropomorphized "intelligence" to which decisions might be outsourced will prove to be problematic when human actors surrender their agency and do not oversee the outputs. The same is true of the "black box" that obscures the specifics of how output is generated and that can create far-reaching yet unintended consequences due to the opaque production of output.

This chapter considers the implications of large language models (LLMs) like ChatGPT as well as other AI-powered systems on the scholarly record, especially since even a healthy suspicion of the anthropomorphized intelligence outputs does not wholly mitigate the black box effect. In this environment, although many kinds of AI are being used in research and writing, the concern will largely center on chatbots. Their ability to craft text seemingly effortlessly, with nothing more than a prompt, has the potential to have far-reaching implications, given the limitations of these systems vis-à-vis the requirements of the scholarly communication ecosystem.

LLMs in Scholarly Writing: Considerations

Scholars have long counted on human actors for support. Well-informed humans can be a reliable and productive source of expertise – if nothing

DOI: 10.4324/9781003570325-5

more, take as evidence the continued roles of the dissertation chair and even the campus writing center in the development of the student as author. Academia continues to be a place where the craft of carrying out and writing up scholarship can be learned and practiced with the oversight and support of subject-area specialists. In other words, academia seems to acknowledge the importance of outside voices to this process and to celebrate their importance in shaping the end product through the mentorship process that has evolved. With LLMs, however, there is no subject area expert or experienced author who deeply understands the user, the nature of the work, the expectations of the field, and the desired end product. And while image generation is useful for creative endeavors, creating images for scholarship is a very different kind of process.

Unreliable Accuracy of Scholarly Outputs

Mistakes are not new, and it can be assumed that humans have been making them for a very long time. Human scholars are certainly not immune to them, as evidenced by the myriad papers eventually retracted over the years due to researcher error. The Retraction Watch Database[3] serves as a mechanism for identifying papers that have been retracted for a wide-ranging number of reasons, including bias issues or lack of balance; concerns/issues about image; error in data; fake peer review; and plagiarism of text. People can be sloppy researchers as well. Anne-Wil Harzing explores the problem of a template for a family of journals being used by authors without removing first the made-up sample reference. The end result is that a "phantom" article has been cited hundreds of times, because authors missed removing the reference, peer reviewers missed that it was a fake article, and copy editors did not notice that the reference was not cited in the paper.[4]

Yet the ease with which errors can be made, and the authority with which they are presented in written products, is amplified by the option to use LLMs as part of the research and writing process. LLMs can easily hallucinate references that sound quite convincing. The phenomenon of reference hallucinations is one that academic librarians working in interlibrary loan quickly came to understand in early 2023. Scholars began to use ChatGPT subsequent to its launch in November 2022 for reviews of the literature. Anecdotally, library staff were frequently scolded by irate professors for not returning the requested articles – articles that seemed 1) legitimate (due to the nature of how LLMs work) and 2) promising for their research. The problem was that these articles simply did not exist, because they were hallucinations of an LLM that was erroneously being used as a search engine.

As mentioned, some degree of control over the outputs can be maintained if the general-purpose LLM is instructed not to hallucinate references, using training data comprised of relevant documents (e.g., articles from a particular field set up as a custom GPT in ChatGPT) or is a purpose-built system designed to work with scholarly sources and to produce scholarly output. One option is to establish a user profile in the general-purpose LLM for the scholar. Another option is to feed copyright-protected articles to the LLM to supplement the corpus. These options should improve the results as well, but at what cost if privacy is surrendered or if protected intellectual property might be retained by a GPT for training, without the author's knowledge or permission?

Lack of Human Creativity

When LLMs create output in response to a prompt, from an intellectual perspective, that output is considered very differently from content created by an individual. The prompt used to elicit the output was, of course, created by an individual and will have a bearing on the way the output is presented. Perceptions of blurred lines between human-authored and AI-generated content can emerge when using AI, confusing notions of agency and ownership.[5] Already, the output of the LLM is based on myriad factors, most of which are obscured by the black box phenomenon. With LLMs, the original texts upon which the output is based are not disclosed. The output will be presented using sterling prose, but even the mechanisms for producing that output are not disclosed.[6]

OpenAI, the firm behind ChatGPT, indicates that ChatGPT output is the publishable property of the creator of the prompt, to be attributed to that individual or company.[7] Legally and ethically, however, this interpretation is not entirely accepted. To be the author of copyrightable text in the US, for example, one has to be sentient, as copyright is tied to human creativity. The US Copyright Office indicates that copyrightable works must be the product of human authorship;[8] in the EU, similar perspectives exist. LLMs cannot be the author of text, then, that is included in a scholarly product like a journal article or a book that is then subsequently copyrighted. This further confounds the scholarly communication process wherein authors adhere to the field's "Authorship Condition" described in Chapter 1 as including the right to priority claims and ownership of work, but also the related responsibilities.

Ethical Concerns With LLM-Authored Texts

LLMs are not capable of meeting authorship requirements in a scholarly communication context.[9] Early after the public release of ChatGPT, a number of articles were indeed published with ChatGPT listed either as a co-author in the byline or as sole author.[10] Many remain, although others have either been retracted or authorship information has been updated. The Retraction Watch blog maintains a list of problematic papers, peer reviews, and author responses to peer reviews that are suspected of using LLMs.[11]

LLMs are particularly susceptible to the ethical concerns for AI raised by Nick Bostrom and Eliezer Yudkowsky in terms of the need for transparency, predictability, security, and a human to act as the responsible party.[12] LLMs can under certain circumstances and in specific journals be listed as a support, with publishers requesting disclosure in the acknowledgments or methodology sections, as appropriate.[13] In other journals:

> AI and AI-assisted technologies should only be used to improve readability and language of the work, and possibly as a 'brain-storm partner', and not be used to carry out the work of the researcher(s) such as producing scientific insights, analyzing and interpreting data, or drawing scientific conclusions.[14]

If used, generative AI (GenAI) tools must not change the substance of images, for example,[15] which otherwise are incredibly easy to fabricate or otherwise falsify using these systems.

For GenAI to be used ethically and with success in writing, the scholarly community needs to establish clearly what is meant by "use" and "misuse" and to be utterly transparent about the ways LLM-authored content has been integrated into the writing process.[16] Ideally, all of the ethical concerns raised by Bostrom and Yudkowsky would be addressed. This is because the use of GenAI in scholarship raises concerns that directly relate to ethics but also to the purpose and function of scholarly communication and the ethos of scholarship in general. Everything presented as requirements in the scholarly communication process needs to be evident in the work produced by GenAI. Yet much of it is absent, presenting a series of ethical concerns about outputs that mimic human intelligence but that are produced through the use of a black box.

Neglecting Topics of Inquiry

When considering possible changes for scholars in the previous chapter, the notion of LLMs "leveling the playing field" was put forth. Hand-in-hand with the question of leveling the playing field for members of marginalized communities is the question of the diversity of topics that marginalized voices wish to address. Emily Bender and colleagues importantly point to the problem of missing topics in LLM training data.[17] Already, a scholarly lack of enthusiasm on the part of the establishment has been identified for topics that 1) are not in vogue in "traditional" scholarly circles, 2) are not able to be fairly vetted by peer reviewers due to the fact that reviewers are largely from the dominant groups, and 3) linguistically might be addressed in other languages but are not widely represented in broader, primarily Anglophone publishing.[18]

An example is the question of topics relevant to individuals living in the Global South.[19] Charlotte Roh, Harrison W. Inefuku, and Emily Drabinski assess some of the literature, describing very limited numbers of journal articles focusing on countries other than the US in economics. What data, then, on the Global South? They also identify the problem of researchers in the Global South opting to study topics that will appeal to editorial boards in the Global North, to the exclusion of topics of local interest. In other words, important and relevant topics are already being excluded from their rightful place in the scholarly record. To make use of LLMs that continue to build exclusively from the limited record that exists essentially enforces these topics' continued exclusion.

Disparate Impact

In the US, *disparate impact* is a policy or practice that appears to be neutral, but in fact, "the policy or practice disproportionately excludes or burdens certain persons on a prohibited basis" such as race.[20] Discrimination due to faulty data analysis is not a novel concept, and disparate impact is not new. For example, Frederick Hoffman, in 1896, citing statistical analysis, claimed that the "gradual extinction [of African Americans] is only a question of time." Part of Hoffman's faulty analysis confused correlation and causation. But by insinuating that African Americans had weak health profiles, Hoffman's work made it difficult for African Americans to obtain health insurance. AI and the black boxes that it represents effortlessly enable classes of individuals to become victims of systems that were trained on faulty data, using algorithms that are not fair, or both.[21]

Facilitating Plagiarism: Presenting LLM-Authored Content as Human-Authored

Because of the functionality of LLMs and the way that tokens are devised and text created, the attribution of ideas cannot be traced.[22] Ideas and text are presented that are not the product of the author's creativity, and their true attribution is not acknowledged or known. This fundamentally limits the ability to follow the trajectory of an idea back to its origin. The problem of not giving credit where credit is due divorces ideas from scholars, which is a fundamental aspect of the scholarly communication process. All told, ethical concerns revolving around the presentation of words and ideas that are not the author's are radically amplified in the face of LLMs.

Education is deeply concerned about the best ways to integrate LLMs into the curriculum so that they are not simply used as engines for academic dishonesty; experienced scholars should not need such oversight, yet at the same time, not all human actors are honest. Indeed, LLMs introduce a scenario where AI-authored content can very easily be presented as having been human-authored; to do so is trivial. The portmanteau term "AIgiarism," or *plagiarism* due to the use of *AI*, has surfaced as a way of talking about the use of LLMs as uncredited coauthors serving up plagiarized content.[23]

Rewritten Versions of an Original Text

Already, LLMs allow unscrupulous actors to create text through the use of prompts, and to do so at little or no cost. At least two scenarios exist where revisions to an existing text can be produced, also at the push of a button, in an attempt to defraud. In the process, the scholarly record is split, with deviations away from the legitimate priority claim via the academic usurper.

LLMs can summarize or reformulate another's work. If published under a new title, with new attribution, it would be difficult to trace the misconduct. To engage in this sort of revision of a text makes the plagiarism invisible to traditional character-by-character plagiarism detectors. Although not a scholarly publishing venue per se, Amazon[24] has been a site where such activities have been observed. Proposals have been made to watermark the content generated by LLMs,[25] but until industry-wide adoption is seen, this will have little impact on the ability of users to inauthentically present content as their own.

Translation into a new language is another way that an idea might be reattributed falsely.[26] Unauthorized translations can be easily made of a source text but with fraudulent attribution. In the past, moving content from one language into another and taking credit was possible, posing problems for collection development in libraries.[27] Such activities were labor-intensive for the translator but were not easily detectable through automated means – another scholar, familiar with the ideas of the original, would likely have to be consulted. Stealing and translating research is easier with LLMs and can take place now at the touch of a button by someone with little to no knowledge of the original language. Due to the language issue and the way most plagiarism detection services work, this kind of misconduct will likewise also go undetected via automated means.

LLM Detection Systems

In an effort to combat the use of LLMs in scholarly writing, AI detection systems have been deployed both in scholarly publishing and in education. None has proven to be particularly effective, though, meaning that at present no fool-proof way to identify LLM-authored content exists. In January 2023, even OpenAI released a detection service called AI classifier but took it offline in less than six months due to accuracy problems.[28]

An interesting side note is that systems to "humanize" AI-generated text by introducing grammatical and typographical errors have flourished – these are intended to help LLM users avoid detection services. ChatGPT currently offers access to a number of these via its custom GPT platform. Other than impacting the scholarly record, these "humanizing" systems might also affect the kinds of products that students submit to their instructors. Such practices 1) have the potential to waste the time of the faculty, who will be providing feedback to a bot's nonsense rather than in support of student development, but also they 2) rob students of the very feedback on their own work that will help them develop critical thinking skills and writing skills, among others. This is because feedback at formative stages of their scholarly careers is assumed to make scholars stronger writers over time.

The current iteration of LLM detectors works in a way that is very different from traditional plagiarism detectors. Traditional plagiarism detectors match strings of text, verbatim. This is great for catching verbatim plagiarism. LLMs, however, provide different outputs based on a corpus in response to a prompt. For medical articles, these yield both high false positive rates, where human-authored academic papers are reported as being LLM-generated, and false negative rates, where LLM-generated academic papers are reported as being human-authored.[29] Although LLM-generated text is well written in terms of grammar and expression, at present it lacks depth, making it indistinguishable from careful and articulate students who have yet to master the nuances of the literature and of expression in the field. What remains to be seen is how aggressively publishers and funders, as well as academic institutions, will require evidence of the non-use of LLMs.

AI and Scholarly Publishing

Research and writing can be made easier with the use of LLMs. If there is an increase in submissions to scholarly publishers because of their use, that has the potential to complicate the work of publishers greatly.[30] This is especially true if the content is unvetted nonsense or slop direct from an LLM. In other words, there are ramifications for flooding the industry with easily generated but worthless content.[31] Regardless, the onus falls on the scholarly publishing community to manage any resulting influx of new articles.

Unsurprisingly, much of the discussion about LLMs in publishing focuses on the mistakes that will undoubtedly be integrated into the scholarly record. The fact that humans are prone to error has not escaped the attention of writers and thinkers in this space.[32] As mentioned in a previous chapter, humans are not infallible when it comes to the errors they introduce, with some mistakes being introduced intentionally, and others being completely unknown to their authors. The question seems to remain, however, whether mistakes that are so easy to generate rapidly and at scale by AI can and should be tolerated. The scholarly publishing community has emphatically decided no, but to put that decision into practice will take a good deal of energy.

Permitting Non-Generative AI Tools for Research

Publishers are generally adopting approaches where non-GenAI tools can be used by scholars in their work but must be declared.[33] For example, *Nature* is currently requesting disclosure in image captions for images or figures that have been manipulated using machine learning (ML) techniques.[34] Non-GenAI tools have consistently been used in support of research. As long as authors continue to be transparent, especially with detailing which tools were used and how, such activities are generally not problematic. Policies regarding the use of non-GenAI can be seen as a continuation of previous approaches to adopting and using technology, including the AI-powered word processing tools that have been actively used in scholarship for a quarter of a century, if not more.

LLMs for Vetting, Reviewing, and Deciding

Optimistic approaches to considering the integration of LLMs into editorial work see the potential for bias to be mitigated. At present, there is a belief among scholars that acceptance of an article into top-tier journals hinges not on the quality of the work, so much as on the gender, seniority, and institutional affiliation of the author(s).[35] Because of the ability of the black box of AI to obscure details about decisions, there is hope that editors will be able to see past information about the authors to focus, instead, on the quality of the piece. However, because of the problematic tendency of AI to replicate all of the biases that already exist in the training data, there is reason to think that the use of LLMs for decision-making in the editorial process will be fraught, favoring those already most favored, thereby contributing to the Matthew effect. To help combat this, journal instructions for editors and reviewers can counsel them not to use LLMs as their only source of evaluation.[36]

Industry-created tools can help editors better analyze reviewer comments and predict a manuscript's suitability for publication. The most promising uses of AI reside in finding ways to identify potential biases at scale, either on the part of reviewers or published papers in the training data, and taking the opportunity to address those biases. In the case of scholars from different language groups or geographical backgrounds, and who might not be addressing questions that are embraced by the mainstream but that are important and compelling, the hope is that these systems will help editors look past biased reviews. Other uses might include helping to reduce initial rejections and summarizing review decisions for editors.[37]

Other uses of AI-powered tools exist as part of the editorial process, and their use should always be judicious. For their part, editors will want to avoid using AI-powered tools as the sole source of data regarding decisions about whether LLMs were used in authoring a manuscript or, insidiously, to predict how well the manuscript will perform if accepted.[38] Editors must also accept final responsibility in identifying reviewers, for example, as the ultimate responsibility for the entire process remains with the scholarly publisher and its agents. In the case of journals, this is the editor.[39]

Peer Reviewer Obligations vis-à-vis LLMs

AI can also affect the work of peer reviewers, ultimately impacting the resulting scholarly record. The effect can be in relation to the use of these systems both by authors and by reviewers. In this way, peer reviewers have the dual responsibility of not falling prey to the well-written prose of LLMs submitted on the part of the purported authors, while they themselves must resist the temptation to use LLMs to pen their reviews.

First, if authored wholly or in part by LLMs, manuscripts risk being both unsound and unethical, and should not become a permanent part of the scholarly record. One problem relating to unsound products of LLMs is the inaccurate references produced as output from ChatGPT, which has been documented,[40] with Joseph Mugaanyi and colleagues finding hallucinations of DOIs in both the natural sciences (61.8%) and the humanities (89.4%) in ChatGPT (GPT-3.5). In their article, DOI hallucinations are defined as DOIs that are either entirely fabricated (i.e., not associated with any source) or inaccurate (i.e., assigned to a different source). There is a difference, though, in the work of researchers such as Mugaanyi and colleagues studying the rate of hallucinations, and the work of peer reviewers, trying to confirm the veracity of sources in papers they have been assigned to review. Already, the accuracy of references and quotations in the peer-reviewed literature has been documented as being problematic well before the ubiquity of LLMs.[41] At the same time, however, LLMs' capacity for creating this kind of error is seemingly endless.

Further, the ease with which generative systems produce text and the confidence with which they write may influence the most vigilant reviewers. Unless both authors and reviewers are aggressive in their fact-checking, AI-produced hallucinations are bound to make their way into the scholarly record via careless and potentially unethical authors. In these cases, hallucinations are unwittingly being codified and becoming part of the scholarly record, presenting myriad problems for the future of the field. In the case of text being created based on a carefully crafted GPT, however, scholars might be able to assemble an exceptional base of articles from which to pull, yielding an authoritative text. Texts authored based on such a GPT might well seem excellently crafted, and due to the authoritative writing style, might as a result fool peer reviewers into accepting them.[42] All told, the scholarly communication system is meant to be trustworthy, built on a traceable flow of ideas. When these sources are confused or misrepresented, that presents formidable challenges for the long-term health of the scholarly record.

Finally, reviewers themselves will need to ensure they are not using LLMs as part of the review process in a way that violates the policies of the journals. *Nature*, for example, does not allow its reviewers to upload manuscripts to ChatGPT for assistance with the evaluation.[43] Other journals and conferences are rejecting LLMs for reviewers as well, with a group of African journals warning reviewers that the use of LLMs violates trust, an integral part of the peer-review process.[44] As previously mentioned, the Retraction Watch blog maintains a list of problematic peer reviews suspected of using LLMs.[45] This list, as the other lists on that page (i.e., papers and author responses) is only expected to grow as time goes on.

Mitigating Editorial Capriciousness

Using AI to help editors is one thing to consider – another is the decision-making process of editors. Decisions made by editors include the decision to consider a manuscript, then sending it to reviewers; another decision is the one to accept or reject a manuscript. Another example is the decision to be made if a journal does not allow LLMs to be used. Concluding whether an LLM has been used to author a text must be done with the utmost care. Such decisions are subjective and can be based on formal or informal criteria for exclusion, including whether a manuscript's author has previously published, whether the author has an email that indicates an institutional affiliation, and whether the work is solo-authored. All of these decisions are particularly prone to discrimination as a kind of *disparate impact*. Just as AI can be trained on faulty training data, decisions to retain or exclude papers based on the sound of an individual's name or the country of origin can unfairly disadvantage legitimate scholars.[46]

Trust in the Scholarly Record Going Forward

As a wide range of sectors find ways to make use of AI, scholarly communication is no exception. The scholarly publishing process involves multiple tasks realized by a variety of actors, from the work of authors when formatting their submissions, to the initial assessments of editors, through to the content of peer reviews to the ways editors interpret them and make decisions.[47] Responsibilities of authorship include assuring accuracy and being owners of the scholarly product, in order to reap the associated rewards. When LLMs produce text, that text is not owned by authors (or by publishers), and the veracity of the text is questionable. Indeed, the sources behind the ideas are completely opaque. What faith, then, can be accorded to the scholarly record going forward?

As the Committee on Publication Ethics (COPE) has explained in the context of vetting manuscripts for consideration that may have been authored by LLMs, "the publishing process is based on trust."[48] Publishers trust their authors, and authors are trustworthy – they must earn the trust they enjoy. Depending on the context, AI can be used in accordance with the tenets of scholarly communication to create works that are trustworthy. The next chapter considers some of the specialized ways the disciplines are using AI, with oversight, to engage in the task of writing with intelligence.

Notes

1 For example, Riccardo Bertolo and Alessandro Antonelli, "Generative AI in Scientific Publishing: Disruptive or Destructive?," *Nature Reviews Urology* 21, no. 1 (January 2024): 1–2, https://doi.org/10.1038/s41585-023-00836-w.
2 Jennifer Chubb, Peter Cowling, and Darren Reed, "Speeding up to Keep up: Exploring the Use of AI in the Research Process," *AI & Society* 37, no. 4 (December 1, 2022): 1439–57, https://doi.org/10.1007/s00146-021-01259-0.
3 "Retraction Watch Database," accessed January 14, 2025, https://retractiondatabase.org/.
4 Anne-Wil Harzing, "The Mystery of the Phantom Reference," *Harzing.Com* (blog), October 26, 2017, https://harzing.com/publications/white-papers/the-mystery-of-the-phantom-reference.
5 Fiona Draxler et al., "The AI Ghostwriter Effect: Users Do Not Perceive Ownership of AI-Generated Text But Self-Declare as Authors," arXiv, March 6, 2023, https://doi.org/10.48550/arXiv.2303.03283.
6 See, for example, the discussion in Heather Moulaison-Sandy and Zach Coble, "Leveraging AI in Cataloging: What Works, and Why?," *Technical Services Quarterly* 41, no. 4 (October 2024): 375–83, https://doi.org/10.1080/07317131.2024.2394912.
7 OpenAI, "Sharing & Publication Policy," accessed March 31, 2023, https://openai.com/policies/sharing-publication-policy#content-co-authored-with-the-open-ai-api.
8 US Copyright Office, "Copyright Registration Guidance: Works Containing Material Generated by Artificial Intelligence," *Federal Register*, March 16, 2023, https://www.federalregister.gov/d/2023-05321.
9 Brian Dobreski, "Author Identities and Artificial Intelligence: Attribution Practices Around the Use of Generative Text Tools," *Journal of Information Ethics* 32, no. 2 (Fall 2023): 42–55, https://doi.org/10.2307/JIE.32.2.42; Brady D. Lund and K. T. Naheem, "Can ChatGPT Be an Author? A Study of Artificial Intelligence Authorship Policies in Top Academic Journals," *Learned Publishing* 37, no. 1 (January 2024): 13–21, https://doi.org/10.1002/leap.1582.
10 For a scholarly discussion, see Andrey A. Popkov and Tyson S. Barrett, "AI vs Academia: Experimental Study on AI Text Detectors' Accuracy in Behavioral Health Academic Writing," *Accountability in Research* (March 22, 2024): 1–17, https://doi.org/10.1080/08989621.2024.2331757.
11 "Papers and Peer Reviews with Evidence of ChatGPT Writing," *Retraction Watch* (blog), March 18, 2024, https://retractionwatch.com/papers-and-peer-reviews-with-evidence-of-chatgpt-writing/.
12 Nick Bostrom and Eliezer Yudkowsky, "The Ethics of Artificial Intelligence," in *The Cambridge Handbook of Artificial Intelligence*, ed. Keith Frankish and William M. Ramsey (Cambridge, UK: Cambridge University Press, 2014), http://assets.cambridge.org/97805218/71426/cover/9780521871426.jpg.
13 Dobreski, "Author Identities and Artificial Intelligence."
14 Caradee Y. Wright et al., "The African Journal Partnership Program's Guidance on the Use of AI in Scholarly Publishing," *Ghana Medical Journal* 58, no. 1 (March 25, 2024): 2, https://doi.org/10.4314/gmj.v58i1.1.

15 Zrinka Pongrac Habdija, "AI in Scholarly Communication," *Food Technology & Biotechnology* 62, no. 1 (2024): 127–29.

16 Ellen Chetwynd, "Ethical Use of Artificial Intelligence for Scientific Writing: Current Trends," *Journal of Human Lactation* 40, no. 2 (May 2024): 211–15, https://doi.org/10.1177/08903344241235160; Eva A. M. van Dis et al., "ChatGPT: Five Priorities for Research," *Nature* 614, no. 7947 (February 9, 2023): 224–26, https://doi.org/10.1038/d41586-023-00288-7.

17 Emily M. Bender et al., "On the Dangers of Stochastic Parrots: Can Language Models Be Too Big? 🦜" (Proceedings of the 2021 ACM Conference on Fairness, Accountability, and Transparency, FAccT '21: 2021 ACM Conference on Fairness, Accountability, and Transparency, Virtual Event Canada: ACM, 2021), 610–23, https://doi.org/10.1145/3442188.3445922.

18 Research on health topics relating to women, for example, are notoriously lacking in the medical literature. Jen Gunter, *The Menopause Manifesto: Own Your Health with Facts and Feminism* (New York, NY: Kensington, 2021).

19 Charlotte Roh, Harrison W. Inefuku, and Emily Drabinski, "Scholarly Communications and Social Justice," in *Reassembling Scholarly Communications*, ed. Martin Paul Eve and Jonathan Gray (MIT Press, 2020), 41–52, https://doi.org/10.7551/mitpress/11885.003.0007.

20 Monika Jansen, "IV. Fair Lending – Fair Lending Laws and Regulations," in *FDIC Consumer Compliance Examination Manual* (FDIC.gov, December 2024), IV–1.3.

21 For example, Cathy O'Neil, *Weapons of Math Destruction: How Big Data Increases Inequality and Threatens Democracy* (Great Britain: Penguin Books, 2017).

22 van Dis et al., "ChatGPT."

23 Mustafa Ali Khalaf, "Does Attitude Towards Plagiarism Predict Algiarism Using ChatGPT?," *AI and Ethics* (February 5, 2024), https://doi.org/10.1007/s43681-024-00426-5.

24 C.f., Kate Knibbs, "Scammy AI-Generated Book Rewrites Are Flooding Amazon," *Wired*, January 10, 2024, https://www.wired.com/story/scammy-ai-generated-books-flooding-amazon/.

25 Sumanth Dathathri et al., "Scalable Watermarking for Identifying Large Language Model Outputs," *Nature* 634, no. 8035 (October 2024): 818–23, https://doi.org/10.1038/s41586-024-08025-4.

26 Jonathan Bailey, "The Problem with Detecting Translated Plagiarism," *Plagiarism Today* (blog), February 24, 2011, https://www.plagiarismtoday.com/2011/02/24/the-problem-with-detecting-translated-plagiarism/.

27 For example, while visiting the library in Alexandria, Egypt, I learned from one of the librarians that collection development in Arabic can be complicated by texts that are, in fact, translations from English to Arabic, with fraudulent attribution in Arabic.

28 "New AI Classifier for Indicating AI-Written Text," accessed November 14, 2024, https://openai.com/index/new-ai-classifier-for-indicating-ai-written-text/.

29 Valentina Bellini et al., "Between Human and AI: Assessing the Reliability of AI Text Detection Tools," *Current Medical Research and Opinion* 40, no. 3 (March 3, 2024): 353–58, https://doi.org/10.1080/03007995.2024.2310086; Popkov and Barrett, "AI vs Academia."

30 Wright et al., "The African Journal Partnership Program's Guidance on the Use of AI in Scholarly Publishing," 2.
31 Gemma Conroy, "How ChatGPT and Other AI Tools Could Disrupt Scientific Publishing," *Nature* 622, no. 7982 (October 12, 2023): 234–36, https://doi.org/10.1038/d41586-023-03144-w.
32 Ethan Mollick, *Co-Intelligence: Living and Working with AI* (New York, NY: Portfolio/Penguin, 2024).
33 Habdija, "AI in Scholarly Communication," 128.
34 Nature, "Artificial Intelligence (AI)," *Editorial Policies*, accessed December 13, 2024, https://www.nature.com/nature/editorial-policies/ai.
35 Neil C. Herndon, "Research Fraud and the Publish or Perish World of Academia," *Journal of Marketing Channels* 23, no. 3 (July 2, 2016): 93, https://doi.org/10.1080/1046669X.2016.1186469.
36 Gregory E. Kaebnick et al., "Editors' Statement on the Responsible Use of Generative AI Technologies in Scholarly Journal Publishing," 53, no. 5 (n.d.): 5, https://doi.org/10.1002/hast.1507.
37 Alessandro Checco et al., "AI-Assisted Peer Review," *Humanities and Social Sciences Communications* 8, no. 1 (January 25, 2021): 25, https://doi.org/10.1057/s41599-020-00703-8.
38 Wright et al., "The African Journal Partnership Program's Guidance on the Use of AI in Scholarly Publishing," 3.
39 Kaebnick et al., "Editors' Statement on the Responsible Use of Generative AI Technologies in Scholarly Journal Publishing," 5.
40 Joseph Mugaanyi et al., "Evaluation of Large Language Model Performance and Reliability for Citations and References in Scholarly Writing: Cross-Disciplinary Study," *Journal of Medical Internet Research* 26 (April 5, 2024): e52935, https://doi.org/10.2196/52935.
41 Helmut A. Abt, "What Fraction of Literature References Are Incorrect?," *Publication of the Astronomical Society of the Pacific* 104 (1992): 235–36; Julianne Awrey et al., "Reference Accuracy in the General Surgery Literature," *World Journal of Surgery* 35, no. 3 (2011): 2014, https://doi.org/10.1007/s00268-010-0912-7; Jon R. Davids et al., "Reference Accuracy in Peer-Reviewed Pediatric Orthopaedic Literature," *The Journal of Bone & Joint Surgery* 92, no. 5 (May 2010): 1155, https://doi.org/10.2106/JBJS.I.00063.
42 van Dis et al., "ChatGPT."
43 Nature, "Artificial Intelligence (AI)," 2024, https://www.nature.com/nature-portfolio/editorial-policies/ai.
44 Wright et al., "The African Journal Partnership Program's Guidance on the Use of AI in Scholarly Publishing," 2.
45 "Papers and Peer Reviews with Evidence of ChatGPT Writing."
46 C.f., COPE, "How to Exclude AI-Generated Articles," *COPE: Committee on Publication Ethics*, 2024, https://publicationethics.org/guidance/case/how-exclude-ai-generated-articles.
47 Kayvan Kousha and Mike Thelwall, "Artificial Intelligence to Support Publishing and Peer Review: A Summary and Review," *Learned Publishing* 37, no. 1 (January 2024): 4–12, https://doi.org/10.1002/leap.1570.
48 COPE, "How to Exclude AI-Generated Articles."

6 Implications for the Disciplines

As AI-powered systems are adopted by scholars, the need to fact-check and otherwise evaluate the output remains, yet with each round of improvements, the systems are performing better. Their use in scholarship is showing more promise than ever.

Supporting Research Tasks

Although different disciplines have different approaches to scholarship, AI-powered tools are able to support work for many scholars. From identifying topics in the sciences, to doing qualitative data analysis in the social sciences, to close investigation of the prose of humanists, applications for AI-powered tools are easy to imagine. As individual scholars decide how AI can enable them to do better research and writing, and as these approaches are taught and learned, the disciplines will continue to grow and evolve as they have through other changes over time.

One of the ways AI-powered tools will help researchers is through the research task, which will look very different from discipline to discipline. Further, write-ups look different as well, meaning that LLMs might be better put to use in some fields more so than others.[1] In this chapter, different approaches that can be adopted are explored with the goal of highlighting how AI, including LLMs, are now changing the research landscape, and how those changes might look going forward, especially as they will be reflected in the scholarly record.

Literature-Based Discovery

One overarching approach to identifying problems is *literature-based discovery* (LBD). LBD is an area of text mining that lends itself to work in the sciences writ large and that, like many of the others mentioned in this chapter, has been around for a long time. It is also a domain that is showing much promise, given the capabilities of AI. For example, LBD might scour the literature for mentions of a particular chemical compound and identify uses,

DOI: 10.4324/9781003570325-6

benefits, drawbacks, and other aspects revealed in the published literature. It can then identify novel uses for that same compound, including in fields unrelated to the ones in which the original research was published. Because it considers published literature broadly, LBD can identify approaches to research that promise to be both new and advantageous, drawing inspiration not from previous work in a single field but rather from all work done, in any field.

At its origins, LBD was not an AI-powered undertaking, since like many of the things AI can help with, LBD can be done manually by humans. Today, LBD relies on AI-powered systems to analyze the breadth of the literature, specifically seeking lacuna and new approaches, focusing often on ones that span disciplines or traditional areas of study.[2] LBD has been generating interest in areas such as medicine and pharmaceuticals,[34] and is seen to be a first step toward automating research entirely.

Increased Interdisciplinary Perspectives

Research in a given discipline will cite other work in that same discipline, including seminal works. One hope for approaches and systems like LBD is that rich relationships will emerge when articles are associated topically instead of based on citing a common body of research (e.g., the "more like this" "content-based recommendations"[5] of recommender systems looking at shared citations). When this happens, interdisciplinary work can follow, inspiring new and interesting ways to look at questions. By allowing AI-powered tools to take research questions out of the silos in which they traditionally reside, interdisciplinary approaches offer compelling ways to work on difficult questions that take inspiration from fields already doing work in those areas.

AI-Powered Advances in STEM Research and Medicine

In research, areas under the science, technology, engineering, and mathematics (STEM) umbrella, including the medical sciences, are able to benefit from AI in powerful ways. As in scholarship more broadly, AI-powered approaches inform idea generation, data collection, and analysis and presentation of results. STEM can make extensive use of other AI-powered tools and systems, too. For lab-based research, universities are pushing out stories about how AI is being put to use on their campuses, with Purdue University, for example, describing how an AI agent manager helps with setting up experiments and analyzing the results.[6] The University of California (UC) Berkeley hosts a website that serves as a portal to descriptions of their many STEM-focused projects using AI.[7] Examples of research grouped under this umbrella involving members of the UC Berkeley community include a machine learning project to model atomistic materials chemistry,[8] and a project to make physics data findable, accessible, interoperable, and reusable (FAIR) and sharable, working toward a platform to enable further discoveries in physics.[9]

Other input such as data from the environment can be analyzed in an automated fashion by AI. As an example, a UC San Diego-based project that is meant to save lives, AlertCalifornia, monitors live camera feeds for natural disasters like fires using AI.[10] The AI being used was developed as a partnership between the California Department of Forestry and Fire Protection (CAL FIRE) and Digital Path, a partner from the private sector. Collaborations among academics have also created a machine learning system to predict earthquake activity,[11] and a deep learning project to predict extreme weather events.[12] In short, the range of STEM-based research that can be supplemented and enhanced by AI is seemingly unlimited.

Finally, in STEM fields, when writing up results, the "strict structure and format requirements"[13] of the writing style lead to formulaic approaches to articles. In producing text that values adherence to the structures of the discipline, the use of LLMs can be especially helpful, especially with routine writing tasks.

Autonomous Experiments and Self-Driving Labs

Another way that AI is empowering new work in STEM and in the so-called *hard sciences*[14] is through the enactment of increasingly autonomous functionalities supporting experimental research. One such example, which is overseen by human researchers, is the increasingly ubiquitous self-driving lab (SDL).

> A self-driving laboratory is comprised of two components: (1) the hardware that automatically prepares the precursors, conducts the experiment, and measures the outcome, and (2) the AI brain (i.e., the data-driven modeling/decision-making strategy), which analyzes the data and autonomously selects the next experiment based on the pre-set objective by a human researcher. The self-driving laboratory serves as an assistant to scientists, who define its objectives as well as initial hypotheses and chemical and physical boundaries.[15]

For example, such labs have been used in chemical and materials sciences,[16] along with LDB for solid-state synthesis of inorganic powders.[17] Each experiment will have an optimal SDL configuration, and considerable effort must go into establishing and enacting it.[18] As with other AI-powered systems, SDLs are quite flawed at present and are in need of human oversight to ensure the quality of the output, yet they show much promise.[19]

Medical Sciences

Although a number of AI-powered tools in medicine are clinical, by nature of the field, approaches using AI also are being piloted, studied, and ultimately written up as part of the scholarly record. They might also be informing approaches for clinicians' efforts to provide better services to patients.[20] For example, the use of machine learning to help diagnose and treat patients with traumatic brain injury has been described in the literature, summarizing work that has been carried out in a hospital setting.[21]

Much potential and much promise exist with a number of cases where the analysis of images or other formats is enhanced through the use of AI, including through LLMs. ChatGPT can, for example, help with the simplification of radiology reports, albeit with potentially biased results.[22] Other work over the past decade or so has looked at ways AI could analyze body language or facial expressions as a way to one day help clinicians diagnose a variety of concerns.[23] There is much to be done going forward, with many aspects of clinical care not yet using AI consistently;[24] the pieces, however, are beginning to fall into place in terms of a critical mass of research and researchers in this space.

Pharmaceuticals

As with all of STEM, pharmaceuticals can and have been leveraging AI in numerous ways for the past 20 years.[25] Some of the aspects most germane to the topic of this book are the ones having to do with research and development (R&D), especially with drug discovery of cancer drugs.[26] As with other areas in the sciences, LDB can be a powerful tool for identifying novel results relating to drug discovery. Drugs' physicochemical properties, bioactivity, and toxicity can be predicted using AI as well. AI can also assist with repurposing existing drugs, which can be efficient for pharmaceutical companies, given that approved drugs have already been proven safe, so the remaining work is to prove they are effective for other purposes.[27]

AI and the Social Sciences

The social sciences stand to benefit from AI in ways that are analogous to STEM and the medical sciences, yet that focus on humans in society rather than compounds, organisms, celestial phenomena, and the other myriad topics addressed in STEM. Mikko Rask and Koki Shimizu, for example, find that LLMs can help with work in the social sciences, not only for the kinds of rote work that the sciences might consider but also for model development.[28] Another way LLMs can be used in the social sciences is for simulating complex social phenomena by creating realistic scenarios for analysis in psychology.[29]

Cultural Studies and History

Cultural studies and history both look at the ways that humans interact with each other, at present and over time. AI is particularly valuable in text-based projects in these areas, including ones with a degree of uncertainty. AI can, for example, be helpful with the automated transcription of lesser-known Semitic languages that are associated with a manuscript tradition like Gəʾəz.[30] Through LLM-powered technology, students of history, with a few caveats, can engage with historical figures via text-based role play, providing LLM-produced insights into the way that Abraham Lincoln, for example, might have reacted to current events based on historical writings and analyses. Although in scenarios where (generally) students are interacting with historical figures, such uses of AI are turning on its head the notion that the humanities are dead. Indeed, many areas of the humanities are fundamentally text-based and their research is as well, and that makes them a particularly good match for LLMs.[31] Specialized systems are emerging, specifically meant to provide LLM-based access to historical figures for students and for anyone wishing to engage with the past through role play.[32]

Education

The acceptability of LLMs in higher education has been debated since the release of ChatGPT in November 2022.[33] With careful and thoughtful use, the benefits are largely seen to outweigh the drawbacks.[34] The potential for LLMs to help with automating interactions between instructors and students is seen as a way for students to have better access to personalized feedback, especially in instances where education is challenging such as in under-resourced environments or large classrooms.[35] AI-powered systems like ChatGPT can help provide individualized feedback to student learners, who otherwise might not have access to personalized results. Systems exist that provide learning analytics (LA), but these systems are often based on computer use, not the content students produce.[36] Instead, based on more qualitative input, a fuller profile of the student learner can be produced. This potentially offers the ability to better meet the student's needs. It can also allow for autonomy on the part of the learner, who is not bound to wait for an instructor before being able to move ahead.[37]

Teaching Test-Takers

One personalized way that LLMs can help is through modeling test taking or giving feedback on practice tests. Already, ChatGPT has successfully taken university-level advanced placement (AP) exams at the high school level[38] and has taken law school exams at the University of Minnesota, where for the most part, it would have received passing grades from the faculty who scored the exams along with the exams of their human students.[39]

Further, LLMs have been very successful at taking and passing written standardized exams, including exams in medicine (such as the multipart US

Medical Licensing Exam (USMLE))[40] and law.[41] In the case of the USMLE, using ChatGPT, Tiffany H. Kung and colleagues found that the LLM passed or nearly passed all three exams:

> AI-generated responses also offered significant insight, role-modeling a deductive reasoning process valuable to human learners. At least one significant insight was present in approximately 90% of outputs. ChatGPT therefore possesses the partial ability to teach medicine by surfacing novel and nonobvious concepts that may not be in learners' sphere of awareness.[42]

Michael J. Bommarito II and Daniel Martin Katz evaluated OpenAI's text-davinci-003 (GPT-3.5) on part of the bar exam offered in the US, finding the LLM to earn a 50% pass rate.[43] Although this project did not seek to use the responses to train test-takers so much as to evaluate the performance of the LLM, there are nonetheless interesting opportunities for future GPTs to continue to improve, producing a sort of custom-made answer key for students as they prepare for high-stakes exams.

AI and the Humanities

The humanities have long been interested in computational techniques, with for example the advent of the digital humanities associated with the beginnings of AI in the 1940s. Digital humanists have made use of AI-powered techniques for their research from at least the 1980s to the present day.[44] These technologies generally require a team of researchers, including contributors with expertise in computer science. Such collaborations are not necessary or even desirable for all humanities projects but represent part of the range of possibilities. Even areas of the humanities that do not align themselves with the digital humanities are nonetheless promoting the use of computational approaches, including AI.[45] In general, though, as Shuo Wang and Hiromi M. Yokoyama indicate, the humanities are writing-intensive fields; as such, scholars may find that concerns naturally arise over their use of LLMs in writing up their research, including the problem that the LLM output will adopt a voice that is not only lacking in humanity but that the output will be fundamentally superficial.[46]

Already, researchers in the humanities support democracy by making individuals "masters of their technology and not its unthinking servants."[47] This is due to the work that humanists do and the questions they ask, and their reach and potential for impact is increasingly pronounced with the advent of AI. As humanists ensure that they remain masters of their technology, new and existing prospects arise for the use of technology as a tool.

Distant Reading and Text-Based Studies

Franco Moretti invited polemics in 2000 when he first described "distant reading" in his article "Conjectures on World Literature."[48] Literary history as a field seeks to "survey patterns that organize human culture."[49] To the consternation of certain scholars, distant reading or the idea of using empirical approaches to study literary history is regularly conflated with the digital humanities.[50] In his article, Moretti proposes an approach to reading text that opposes the close reading of a limited number of sources in a specific language. He instead suggests looking more broadly at areas outside of, or existing alongside, the text: "devices, themes, tropes – or genres and systems."[51] Not dissimilar to a kind of literary LBD, this approach allows for insight into overarching topics or themes that emerge across world literatures, with Moretti giving as an example a similar theme in Japanese and Indian novels, with that same theme also emerging in Brazil.

Although close reading tends to still be the purview of human scholars, AI and NLP can help with approaches that survey a large number of texts at scale, or the *big data* of literature.[52] The concept of distant reading has been applied outside of literary history to the broader use of NLP in analyzing other kinds of texts, including in the case of Martin Paul Eve and colleagues, peer reviews of scholarship.[53] AI can also be used to perform unexpected analyses of modern literature. Ying Yuan, for example, uses AI to analyze the personalities of characters in Chinese novels using an established system for psychoanalysis.[54]

Ancient texts can likewise be analyzed using AI. An AI-powered project using *algorithmic historians*[55] has been successful at automatic transcriptions of handwritten historical documents in Spanish.[56] In addition, AI-powered products such as Ithaca, a deep neural network, are able to make sense of damaged ancient Greek inscriptions, filling in missing letters and words as it supplements human-based work in epigraphy. Ithaca can also provide information about the geographical origins of an inscription as well as information about when it was created, outperforming human experts in the process.[57]

Book History

As the printed word has evolved from being primarily handwritten to being primarily printed, the need to understand elements of books has also evolved. Julia Thomas and Irene Testini describe an AI-powered system that has been created to help identify image captions in over a million image scans of 68,000 books published between the 18th and early 20th centuries. Although somewhat standardized today, "[t]he very presence of captions varies considerably across historical book illustrations" making this an area of study that was able to benefit from the application of AI-powered tools.[58] A wealth of other projects exist, including one to analyze printing technology (e.g., lithography) through the use of deep learning methods.[59]

There is a good deal of potential in the book history and print culture space as well. Another project, one to build an AI-powered system to analyze historical bookbindings, is still in the phase of being conceptualized.[60] Marginalia and other idiosyncratic elements of certain physical copies of historical manuscripts are not, however, available for consideration by LLMs, leading at least one Victorian literature scholar to insist on the continued importance of *analog intelligence*.[61] In the humanities, the two intelligences will surely exist in parallel for the foreseeable future.

Art History

With AI-powered tools, *algorithmic art historians* and the like can also be envisioned.[62] One example is the work presented by Tomas Jenicek and Ondřej Chum, where scanned artworks are compared, and human figure depiction, from the perspective of pose similarity, is identified. This system, OpenPose, outperforms current image retrieval systems as well as manual ones.[63] Similar work has successfully been carried out to analyze head poses.[64] Individual paintings can also be analyzed with AI. For example, a close analysis of Jan Vermeer's *Girl with a Pearl Earring* revealed that the light source was consistently represented, affirming that Vermeer painted from a model.[65]

Creating and Co-Creating With AI

Authoring and co-authoring with GenAI systems has proven to be helpful in enhancing human creativity.[66] Researchers have developed systems where LLMs coauthor stories, working with writers to help with ideas and phrasing. Users report feelings of ownership for the resulting text.[67] This might not be surprising if Blaise Cronin's notion is kept in mind, that "[t]he humanities have been more fluid in their approach to authorship"[68] and that fiction writing seems to be governed by these same ideas. Indeed, the humanities are a locus for exploration and use of AI-powered systems, as well as test cases (both artistically and legally). Text invites this kind of play, with LLMs proving to be compelling muses (and coauthors) for certain authors. Alice Hei, for example, published a short story in the *New Yorker* that she coauthored with an LLM called Chai AI.[69]

Creations are not confined to text, as GenAI is also able to create images as well as audio in response to prompts. These affordances have been used by artists in their work, with an extreme example of GenAI use being an entire 2021 graphic novel's images and text being created by a GPT-3 system.[70] Another example is the creation of an art installation at the Museum of Modern Art (MOMA) in New York by Refik Anadol, where Anadol built his own AI model and ran the artworks of the MOMA through it, with the output as his exhibit.[71] Although these systems will not always perform well in creating images to correspond to specialized prompts such as the text of a proverb in a particular language,[72] they can create compelling images in response to otherwise simple prompts.[73] In addition, music is another domain in which human creativity can be supplemented with the use of GenAI. Holly Herndon[74] describes some of her current work producing music via AI in the *New Yorker*. Herndon is convinced that music is as relevant today as it was in the era of Bach and Beethoven, and that AI should be trained on and deployed not only in relation to musical forms of the past but also the present, which she has done.[75]

Concerns With Outsourcing "Intelligence"

The disciplines and the individuals working within them will have to make sense of the best ways to use AI-powered tools, if at all. The effect on junior scholars and students still being educated is less clear, with a lot of strong opinions being voiced. Two such points are the problem of developing creativity in scholars going forward and ensuring they have the critical thinking skills to do the needed work.

Impact on Human Creativity

Concerns about the impact of the use of GenAI tools on human creativity have been raised. One camp is concerned that generations of researchers will be poorly trained due to their reliance on LLMs. This group sees LLMs as diminishing human creativity and also critical thinking[76] in scholarly writing processes. For Wang and Yokoyama, the concerns are especially noteworthy for humanists for whom "writing is research, and research is writing."[77] Such concerns seem to echo the voices of those who, over the years, have identified technologies that have the potential to change habits and, by the same token, values and behaviors. At the same time, there is an expectation that practices and behaviors will change and shift over the years in light of new technologies. With concerns about writing skills diminishing, given the use of LLMs as a point of departure for essays, instructors are warned against only teaching "students how to be great editors of AI-written content,"[78] urging them instead to ensure that students continue to be able to channel their own innate creativity when faced with a blank page.

An Impending Crisis in Critical Thinking Skills?

Indeed, the question of using AI, but especially LLMs, as part of the training of future researchers and scholars invites polemics. In one camp are those who fear that the use of systems like ChatGPT is leading to the decline of critical thinking skills. If critical thinking is defined as John Dewey first did in 1910 to imply both cognitive and affective components,[79] then LLMs are fundamentally incapable of critical thinking. The question, then, is the extent to which users of these systems are deprived of the opportunity to develop their own critical thinking skills.

Depending on the source (and the context), caution is being counseled in the face of LLMs and their use by students. This is especially true for their use by primary and secondary school students who will, it is argued, no longer possess the necessary critical thinking skills by the time they arrive at their chosen institution of higher education.[80] Informal comparisons of ChatGPT to human-authored text have come up wanting, concluding that LLMs produce "lazy knowledge."[81] The opposite can also be said to be true, however, with other scholars like Rossella Suriano and colleagues finding that the use of LLMs in teaching can actually promote critical thinking skills.[82] A Master's thesis written by a student at the Massachusetts Institute of Technology (MIT), Valdemar M. Danry, considers how AI-enhanced reasoning systems can have a positive impact on critical thinking skills.[83] Researchers in education have promoted findings that reinforce the usefulness of LLMs to critical thinking skills, with the caveat that the instruction include training in what might be termed information literacy.[84]

It is difficult, however, to see how consuming nonsense written by an LLM differs from being greeted regularly by misinformation online. There is a crisis surrounding misinformation, and not all of it is produced confidently by an LLM in response to a user's prompt – some of it appears online courtesy of nefarious or naïve actors. Information literacy and critical thinking skills are surely as much a part of modern life as the internet and ChatGPT. For this, scholars in the area of information literacy will not be at a loss for work, nor will the scholars and learners who will need to make sense of their respective fields and the affordances and drawbacks of AI going forward.

Next, the final chapter in this book looks at ways that improvements to AI might affect scholarship, from the activities of scholars to new fields of study. AI also has the potential to change scholarly communication in meaningful ways.

Notes

1 For example, Wang Shuo and Hiromi M. Yokoyama., "Fight Fire with Fire: Why Not Be More Tolerant of ChatGPT in Academic Writing?" *AI & SOCIETY*, July 27, 2024, https://doi.org/10.1007/s00146-024-02025-8.

2 Neil R. Smalheiser, "Literature-Based Discovery: Beyond the ABCs," *Journal of the American Society for Information Science and Technology* 63, no. 2 (2012): 218–24, https://doi.org/10.1002/asi.21599; Thilakaratne, Falkner, and Atapattu, "A Systematic Review on Literature-Based Discovery."

3 For example, Sudha Cheerkoot-Jalim and Kavi Kumar Khedo, "Literature-Based Discovery Approaches for Evidence-Based Healthcare: A Systematic

Review," *Health and Technology* 11, no. 6 (November 2021): 1205–17, https://doi.org/10.1007/s12553-021-00605-y; Thilakaratne, Falkner, and Atapattu, "A Systematic Review on Literature-Based Discovery."

4 For example, Debleena Paul et al., "Artificial Intelligence in Drug Discovery and Development," *Drug Discovery Today* 26, no. 1 (October 21, 2020): 80, https://doi.org/10.1016/j.drudis.2020.10.010.

5 Robin Burke, Alexander Felfernig, and Mehmet H. Göker, "Recommender Systems: An Overview," *AI Magazine* 32, no. 3 (June 5, 2011): 13–18, https://doi.org/10.1609/aimag.v32i3.2361; Qian Zhang, Jie Lu, and Yaochu Jin, "Artificial Intelligence in Recommender Systems," *Complex & Intelligent Systems* 7, no. 1 (February 1, 2021): 439–57, https://doi.org/10.1007/s40747-020-00212-w.

6 Mary Martialay, "Accelerating Scientific and Drug Discovery in an AI-Powered Lab," *Research at Purdue* (blog), April 26, 2024, https://www.purdue.edu/research/features/stories/accelerating-scientific-and-drug-discovery-in-an-ai-powered-lab/.

7 "AI Projects," *Lawrence Berkeley National Laboratory*, accessed November 12, 2024, https://www.lbl.gov/ai-projects/.

8 Ilyes Batatia et al., "A Foundation Model for Atomistic Materials Chemistry," arXiv, March 1, 2024, https://doi.org/10.48550/arXiv.2401.00096.

9 Wahid Bhimji et al., "FAIR Universe HiggsML Uncertainty Challenge Competition," arXiv, October 3, 2024, https://doi.org/10.48550/arXiv.2410.02867.

10 "How California Is Using AI to Spot Wildfires before They Start," 2024, https://www.cnn.com/2024/10/21/world/video/innovate-california-wildfires-ai-spc.

11 Dongwei Lyu et al., "WaveCastNet: An AI-Enabled Wavefield Forecasting Framework for Earthquake Early Warning," arXiv, May 30, 2024, https://doi.org/10.48550/arXiv.2405.20516.

12 "Perlmutter-Powered Deep-Learning Model Speeds Extreme Weather Predictions – Computing Sciences News Archive," accessed November 12, 2024, https://cs-newsarchive.lbl.gov/news/perlmutter-powered-deep-learning-model-speeds-extreme-weather-predictions/.

13 Wang and Yokoyama, "Fight Fire with Fire," 1–2.

14 The hard sciences can be differentiated from the social sciences and humanities through their emphasis on empirical methodologies, and their objective analysis of quantitative data. Examples include physics, chemistry, biology, earth sciences, and astronomy.

15 Robert W. Epps et al., "Universal Self-Driving Laboratory for Accelerated Discovery of Materials and Molecules," *Chem* 7, no. 10 (October 2021): 2541, https://doi.org/10.1016/j.chempr.2021.09.004.

16 Milad Abolhasani and Eugenia Kumacheva, "The Rise of Self-Driving Labs in Chemical and Materials Sciences," *Nature Synthesis* 2, no. 6 (June 2023): 483–92, https://doi.org/10.1038/s44160-022-00231-0.

17 Nathan J. Szymanski et al., "An Autonomous Laboratory for the Accelerated Synthesis of Novel Materials," *Nature* 624, no. 7990 (December 2023): 86–91, https://doi.org/10.1038/s41586-023-06734-w.

18 Amanda A. Volk and Milad Abolhasani, "Performance Metrics to Unleash the Power of Self-Driving Labs in Chemistry and Materials Science,"

Nature Communications 15, no. 1 (February 14, 2024): 1378, https://doi.org/10.1038/s41467-024-45569-5.

19 Zhichu Ren et al., "Autonomous Experiments Using Active Learning and AI," *Nature Reviews Materials* 8, no. 9 (August 3, 2023): 563–64, https://doi.org/10.1038/s41578-023-00588-4.

20 For example, Junaid Bajwa et al., "Artificial Intelligence in Healthcare: Transforming the Practice of Medicine," *Future Healthcare Journal* 8, no. 2 (July 2021): e188, https://doi.org/10.7861/fhj.2021-0095.

21 Andrew Tritt et al., "Data-Driven Distillation and Precision Prognosis in Traumatic Brain Injury with Interpretable Machine Learning," *Scientific Reports* 13, no. 1 (December 1, 2023): 21200, https://doi.org/10.1038/s41598-023-48054-z.

22 Kanhai S. Amin, Howard P. Forman, and Melissa A. Davis, "Even with ChatGPT, Race Matters," *Clinical Imaging* 109 (May 2024): 110113, https://doi.org/10.1016/j.clinimag.2024.110113.

23 Rawad Abdulghafor et al., "An Analysis of Body Language of Patients Using Artificial Intelligence," *Healthcare* 10, no. 12 (December 2022): 2504, https://doi.org/10.3390/healthcare10122504.

24 Tiffany H. Kung et al., "Performance of ChatGPT on USMLE: Potential for AI-Assisted Medical Education Using Large Language Models," ed. Alon Dagan, *PLoS Digital Health* 2, no. 2 (February 9, 2023): 2, https://doi.org/10.1371/journal.pdig.0000198.

25 Sheela Kolluri et al., "Machine Learning and Artificial Intelligence in Pharmaceutical Research and Development: A Review," *The AAPS Journal* 24, no. 1 (January 2022): 19, https://doi.org/10.1208/s12248-021-00644-3.

26 Solene Bechelli and Jerome Delhommelle, "AI's Role in Pharmaceuticals: Assisting Drug Design from Protein Interactions to Drug Development," *Artificial Intelligence Chemistry* 2, no. 1 (June 1, 2024): 100038, https://doi.org/10.1016/j.aichem.2023.100038; Paul et al., "Artificial Intelligence in Drug Discovery and Development."

27 Paul et al., "Artificial Intelligence in Drug Discovery and Development."

28 Mikko Rask and Koki Shimizu, "Beyond the Average: Exploring the Potential and Challenges of Large Language Models in Social Science Research" (2024 International Conference on Artificial Intelligence, Computer, Data Sciences and Applications (ACDSA), 2024 International Conference on Artificial Intelligence, Computer, Data Sciences and Applications (ACDSA), Victoria, Seychelles: IEEE, 2024), 1–5, https://doi.org/10.1109/ACDSA59508.2024.10467341.

29 Burak Senel, *Exploring ChatGPT in Research and Education* (SAGE Publications Inc., August 25, 2023), https://us.sagepub.com/en-us/nam/exploring-chatgpt-in-research-and-education.

30 Samuel Grieggs et al., "Automated Transcription of Gə'əz Manuscripts Using Deep Learning," *Digital Humanities Quarterly* 17, no. 3 (2023), https://www.digitalhumanities.org/dhq/vol/17/3/000682/000682.html.

31 Benjamin Breen, "Simulating History with ChatGPT," *Substack Newsletter, Res Obscura* (blog), September 12, 2023, https://resobscura.substack.com/p/simulating-history-with-chatgpt.

32 Jessica Stewart, "AI Chatbots Now Let You Talk to Historical Figures Like Shakespeare and Andy Warhol," *My Modern Met* (blog), accessed

November 5, 2024, https://platform.tumblr.com/v2/follow_button.html?type=follow&tumblelog=mymodernmet&color=blue; David Ingram, "Chatbot That Lets You Talk to Jesus and Hitler is Latest AI Controversy," *NBC News*, January 20, 2023, https://www.nbcnews.com/tech/tech-news/chatgpt-gpt-chat-bot-ai-hitler-historical-figures-open-rcna66531.

33 Benjamin Luke Moorhouse, Marie Alina Yeo, and Yuwei Wan, "Generative AI Tools and Assessment: Guidelines of the World's Top-Ranking Universities," *Computers and Education Open* 5 (December 15, 2023): 100151, https://doi.org/10.1016/j.caeo.2023.100151.

34 Grace H. Sun and Stephanie H. Hoelscher, "The ChatGPT Storm and What Faculty Can Do," *Nurse Educator* 48, no. 3 (June 2023): 119, https://doi.org/10.1097/NNE.0000000000001390.

35 Yun Dai, Ang Liu, and Cher Ping Lim, "Reconceptualizing ChatGPT and Generative AI as a Student-Driven Innovation in Higher Education," *Procedia CIRP* 119 (2023): 86, https://doi.org/10.1016/j.procir.2023.05.002.

36 Dai, Liu, and Lim, "Reconceptualizing ChatGPT and Generative AI as a Student-Driven Innovation in Higher Education," 85.

37 Dai, Liu, and Lim, "Reconceptualizing ChatGPT and Generative AI as a Student-Driven Innovation in Higher Education," 86.

38 Joanna Stern, "ChatGPT Wrote My AP English Essay – and I Passed," *Wall Street Journal, SEC. Tech*, December 21, 2022, https://www.wsj.com/articles/chatgpt-wrote-my-ap-english-essayand-i-passed−11671628256.

39 Karen Sloan, "ChatGPT Passes Law School Exams Despite 'Mediocre' Performance," *Reuters, SEC. Transactional*, January 25, 2023, https://www.reuters.com/legal/transactional/chatgpt-passes-law-school-exams-despite-mediocre-performance-2023-01-25/.

40 Kung et al., "Performance of ChatGPT on USMLE."

41 Michael James Bommarito and Daniel Martin Katz, "GPT Takes the Bar Exam" (SSRN Scholarly Paper, Rochester, NY, December 29, 2022), https://doi.org/10.2139/ssrn.4314839.

42 Kung et al., "Performance of ChatGPT on USMLE," 9.

43 Bommarito and Katz, "GPT Takes the Bar Exam."

44 Ding-Yu Wang et al., "Artificial Intelligence Suppression as a Strategy to Mitigate Artificial Intelligence Automation Bias," *Journal of the American Medical Informatics Association* 30, no. 10 (October 1, 2023): 1684–92, https://doi.org/10.1093/jamia/ocad118.

45 For example, the National Humanities Center, located in North Carolina, USA, sponsored a conference in 2021 (prior to the release of ChatGPT) entitled *In Our Image*. Recordings of the presentations as well as podcasts, a bibliography, and a resource for teaching: https://nationalhumanitiescenter.org/in-our-image-ai-humanities/.

46 For example, Wang and Yokoyama, "Fight Fire with Fire," 1–2.

47 "Title 20 – Education," in *Chapter 26-Support and Scholarship in Humanities and Arts; Museum Services Subchapter I-National Foundation on the Arts and the Humanities United States Code § 951 – Declaration of Findings and Purposes* (2018), para. 4, https://www.govinfo.gov/content/pkg/USCODE-2018-title20/html/USCODE-2018-title20-chap26-subchapI-sec951.htm.

48 Franco Moretti, "Conjectures on World Literature," *New Left Review* 2, no. 1 (2000): 54–68.
49 Ted Underwood, "A Genealogy of Distant Reading," *Digital Humanities Quarterly* 11, no. 2 (2017): para. 5, https://www-proquest-com.proxy.mul.missouri.edu/docview/2555196599?fromopenview=true&pq-origsite=gscholar&sourcetype=Scholarly%20Journals.
50 Underwood, "A Genealogy of Distant Reading."
51 Moretti, "Conjectures on World Literature," 57.
52 Underwood, "A Genealogy of Distant Reading."
53 For example, Martin Paul Eve et al., *Reading Peer Review*, 1st ed. (Cambridge University Press, 2020), https://doi.org/10.1017/9781108783521.
54 Ying Yuan, "Analysis of Fictional Characters in the Context of Artificial Intelligence and Big Data: Taking A Dream of Red Mansions for Example," *Digital Scholarship in the Humanities* 37, no. 1 (April 1, 2022): 289–97, https://doi.org/10.1093/llc/fqab064; Ying Yuan, "Research on the Psychology of Fictional Characters Based on Artificial Intelligence – an Example Study on The Family," *Digital Scholarship in the Humanities* 38, no. 2 (June 1, 2023): 798–806, https://doi.org/10.1093/llc/fqac058.
55 Elsa González-Esteban and Patrici Calvo, "Ethically Governing Artificial Intelligence in the Field of Scientific Research and Innovation," *Heliyon* 8, no. 2 (February 2022): e08946, https://doi.org/10.1016/j.heliyon.2022.e08946.
56 E. Vidal et al., "The Carabela Project and Manuscript Collection: Large-Scale Probabilistic Indexing and Content-Based Classification" (2020 17th International Conference on Frontiers in Handwriting Recognition (ICFHR), 2020), 85–90, https://doi.org/10.1109/ICFHR2020.2020.00026.
57 Yannis Assael et al., "Restoring and Attributing Ancient Texts Using Deep Neural Networks," *Nature* 603, no. 7900 (March 2022): 280–83, https://doi.org/10.1038/s41586-022-04448-z.
58 Julia Thomas and Irene Testini, "Capturing Captions: Using AI to Identify and Analyse Image Captions in a Large Dataset of Historical Book Illustrations," *Digital Humanities Quarterly* 18, no. 2 (2024): 2–16, https://www.digitalhumanities.org/dhq/vol/18/2/000740/000740.html.
59 Chanjong Im, Yongho Kim, and Thomas Mandl, "Deep Learning for Historical Books: Classification of Printing Technology for Digitized Images," *Multimedia Tools and Applications* 81, no. 4 (February 2022): 5867–88, https://doi.org/10.1007/s11042-021-11754-7.
60 María Helena Vargas Mejía, "Perspectives on the Identification and Description with Artificial Intelligence for Open Access Data of Artistic Historical Bookbindings for Researchers," *ILCEA*, no. 39 (March 3, 2020), https://doi.org/10.4000/ilcea.9066.
61 Andrew M. Stauffer, "Analog Intelligence," *Victorian Poetry* 61, no. 4 (December 2024): 553–60, https://doi.org/10.1353/vp.2024.a933705. David G. Stork, "How AI Is Expanding Art History," *Nature* 623, no. 7988 (November 21, 2023): 685–87, https://doi.org/10.1038/d41586-023-03604-3.
62 González-Esteban and Calvo, "Ethically Governing Artificial Intelligence in the Field of Scientific Research and Innovation."

63 Tomas Jenicek and Ondřej Chum, "Linking Art through Human Poses," arXiv, July 8, 2019, https://doi.org/10.48550/arXiv.1907.03537.
64 Jean-Peïc Chou and David G. Stork, "Computational Tracking of Head Pose through 500 Years of Fine-Art Portraiture," *Electronic Imaging* 35 (January 16, 2023): 1–13, https://doi.org/10.2352/EI.2023.35.13.CVAA−211.
65 Micah K. Johnson et al., "Inferring Illumination Direction Estimated from Disparate Sources in Paintings: An Investigation into Jan Vermeer's Girl with a Pearl Earring," in *Computer Image Analysis in the Study of Art*, vol. 6810 (SPIE, 2008), 164–75, https://doi.org/10.1117/12.759726.
66 For example, Mirko Farina et al., "Machine Learning in Human Creativity: Status and Perspectives," *AI & Society* (January 12, 2024), https://doi.org/10.1007/s00146-023-01836-5.
67 Yuan et al., "Wordcraft."
68 Blaise Cronin, "Collaboration in Art and in Science: Approaches to Attribution, Authorship, and Acknowledgment," *Information & Culture* 47, no. 1 (2012): 32.
69 Sheila Heti, "'According to Alice,' by Sheila Heti," *The New Yorker*, November 13, 2023, https://www.newyorker.com/magazine/2023/11/20/according-to-alice-fiction-sheila-heti.
70 "Fastwalkers," *Ilan Manouach* (blog), accessed November 11, 2024, https://ilanmanouach.com/work/fastwalkers/.
71 Matt O'Brien, "AI Tools Can Create New Images, but Who Is the Real Artist?," *AP News*, January 19, 2023, https://apnews.com/article/artificial-intelligence-images-rights-1c6d9e0e260e2d135a3e3bf98d5493df.
72 Luis J. Tosina Fernández, "Proverbs as Indicators of Proficiency for Art-Generating AI," *Digital Scholarship in the Humanities* 38, no. 3 (September 1, 2023): 1296–306, https://doi.org/10.1093/llc/fqad034.
73 Mollick shows a charming example of a hand drawn image of an airplane surrounded by hearts and the quite sophisticated GenAI interpretation of the same idea. Ethan Mollick, *Co-Intelligence: Living and Working with AI* (New York, NY: Portfolio/Penguin, 2024).
74 Minhyang (Mia) Suh et al., "AI as Social Glue: Uncovering the Roles of Deep Generative AI during Social Music Composition," in *Proceedings of the 2021 CHI Conference on Human Factors in Computing Systems, CHI '21* (New York, NY, USA: Association for Computing Machinery, 2021), 1–11, https://doi.org/10.1145/3411764.3445219; Cheng-Zhi Anna Huang et al., "AI Song Contest: Human-AI Co-Creation in Songwriting," arXiv, October 12, 2020, https://doi.org/10.48550/arXiv.2010.05388.
75 Anna Wiener, "Holly Herndon's Infinite Art," *The New Yorker*, November 13, 2023, https://www.newyorker.com/magazine/2023/11/20/holly-herndons-infinite-art.
76 For example, Enrique Dans, "ChatGPT and the Decline of Critical Thinking," *IE Insights* (blog), January 27, 2023, https://www.ie.edu/insights/articles/chatgpt-and-the-decline-of-critical-thinking/; Wang and Yokoyama, "Fight Fire with Fire."
77 Wang and Yokoyama, "Fight Fire with Fire," 1–2.
78 Ben Civil, "ChatGPT Can Hinder Students' Critical Thinking Skills," *The Journal*, March 17, 2023, https://www.queensjournal.ca/story/2023-03-16/opinions/chatgpt-can-hinder-students-critical-thinking-skills/.

79 Barbara Z. Larson et al., "Critical Thinking in the Age of Generative AI," *Academy of Management Learning & Education* 23, no. 3 (September 2024): 373–78, https://doi.org/10.5465/amle.2024.0338.

80 For example, Larson et al. "Critical Thinking in the Age of Generative AI."

81 Dirk Lindebaum and Peter Fleming, "ChatGPT Undermines Human Reflexivity, Scientific Responsibility and Responsible Management Research," *British Journal of Management* 35, no. 2 (2024): 573, https://doi.org/10.1111/1467-8551.12781.

82 Rossella Suriano et al., "Student Interaction with ChatGPT Can Promote Complex Critical Thinking Skills," *Learning and Instruction* 95 (February 1, 2025): 102011, https://doi.org/10.1016/j.learninstruc.2024.102011.

83 Valdemar M. Danry, "AI Enhanced Reasoning: Augmenting Human Critical Thinking with AI Systems" (Thesis, Massachusetts Institute of Technology, 2023), https://dspace.mit.edu/handle/1721.1/151971.

84 Suriano et al., "Student Interaction with ChatGPT Can Promote Complex Critical Thinking Skills."

7 Future Trends and Prospects for Scholarly Communication

One thing that can be predicted with near certainty is that AI technologies will continue to improve, and dramatically, into the future. AI that has been dreamed of but not yet accomplished today will almost certainly be successfully completed tomorrow. With these changes to technology being predictable, one part of the equation regarding the future of AI and scholarly communication is somewhat easily advanced – this wording is redundant, and a little confusing as a result that AI will influence scholarship is all but assured.

One wild card in this scenario is the actors in the scholarly publishing ecosystem themselves. Behavior seems to be changing already on the part of scholars, at least on the parts of some, pertaining to their willingness to use or even their expectations regarding the use of large language models (LLMs). For evidence of this, there is no need to go further than the websites of scholarly journals instructing authors to please acknowledge their use of LLMs (or forbidding the use of LLMs entirely) and instructing peer reviewers not to use them at all, lest the intellectual property of the manuscript owners (and possibly the future intellectual property of the journal itself) become grist for the LLM mill. Yet how much scholars will be willing to adapt their practices, and their continued tolerance for doing labor-intensive work manually, remains to be seen.

From the point of departure of the standards and practices that are the hallmark of the scholarly communication process, this chapter considers the changing perspectives as further adoption of these tools across the spectrum of scholarly communication activities takes place. It also considers some ways that AI is changing fields that already exist. Focusing on what is established about scholarly communication and the potential for using these systems going forward, this chapter concludes by considering some possible changes in perspective on the horizon for scholarly communication in the era of AI.

Scholars' Changing Approaches to AI

As scholars become increasingly comfortable with AI, their expectations and behaviors are shifting. For some, these changes will be more pronounced than

DOI: 10.4324/9781003570325-7

for others. Some scholars, for example, might find themselves partnering with AI-powered tools as a way of further facilitating their work, whereas others might outsource their work entirely.

Sharing the Workload

Stereotypes of scholars include both solo geniuses writing into the night and collaborative groups of enthusiasts working to solve problems. Rarely do these stereotypes include assistants ready to do their bidding, but conceptualizations of AI that foresee a greater role in scholarly communication are promising just that. A variety of AI-powered systems, once perfected, will be key to producing a single AI assistant that serves as a reliable, all-in-one resource. One might imagine an AI assistant ready, willing, and able to help with all aspects of the research and writing process, including ones that facilitate the technical aspects of the work, and ones that connect and align human actors as they reflect, engage, and communicate with each other.[1] In an environment where humans and AI share the load, AI can be perfected in the kinds of research and writing support roles already described in this book. The AI assistant sharing the load, however, will go above and beyond by anticipating needs and suggesting the best solutions to its human partners.

A glimpse at the promise of AI assistants is being teased by systems already on the market. Microsoft has branded its AI-powered productivity tool "Copilot" – this tool is integrated with general productivity software such as word processing and email. The intention is that the AI system and the human author will work in tandem, ostensibly with the software providing support and the human making the final decision. Licensed by some universities, Copilot claims to be able to assist scholars with literature reviews, writing assistance, data analysis, citation management, proofreading and editing, finding journals as venues for publication, responding to peer reviewers and making the requested edits, and current awareness services. The extent to which any of these items is accomplished well will depend on the perspective of the researcher, but all told, a bit of help is likely better than none at all, at least on some of these counts.

For specific research-related tasks, AI assistants will also be able to pitch in meaningfully to the work of their human stewards. For example, AI is well-suited to writing code.[2] Beyond Copilot, other AI-powered systems able to create code from natural language prompts include specialized services such as Codex from OpenAI and the system AlphaCode from Google Alphabet, which has performed at a competitive level.[3] These companies envision a future where human programmers and AI-powered tools work together.[4] In time, as with other systems where AI is currently sharing the load, the work should require less and less human supervision, and is quickly becoming the purview of these specialized systems.[5]

As the actors in the scholarly publishing ecosystem, from researchers and authors to publishers and editors, become increasingly acquainted with the affordances of AI-powered technologies on offer, they will increasingly expect to use them. As AI improves, normalizing its use in a way that places it as a member of the research team will help scholars to continue to make their work better, more efficient, and more impactful.

Or the End of the Human Scientist?

The availability of increasingly performant AI systems has led scholars to wonder about the possibility of outsourcing the entirety of the scientific enterprise to so-called "AI scientists" at least in the *hard sciences*.[6] How might this work? Intuition has previously guided research[7] but with the increasing use of AI in scientific research and the advent of the exciting possibility of the AI scientist,[8] that could be changing. For example, the 2023 US National Academies workshop on AI in scientific discovery[9] featured speakers who presented ideas about the feasibility of independent AI scientists (versus human scientists) who could run their own labs, carrying out their own research through the use of specialized software and hardware such as robots and sensors.[10]

Like the envisioned AI assistants, AI scientists will use a mash-up of existing AI-based technologies, all of which are imperfect at present but improving all the time. They might start a project by carrying out literature-based discovery (LBD) using AI-based systems to identify important questions that the literature has not yet addressed. They could then establish research methods based on previous work described in the literature. With the use of robots and sensors, they could then run experiments and collect data using self-driving labs (SDL) while maintaining the lab. The whole of the work could be overseen by a kind of autonomous AI manager, a perfected and integrated version of the systems described in the previous section on sharing the load, overseeing the entire process and its evaluation, and going on to share the results with researchers in the form of scholarly articles.

In other words, like the AI assistant, the AI scientist is close, and many of the pieces are already in place. As it stands, though, the advent of the AI scientist creates new problems, as even once its work is perfected, the AI scientist cannot author scholarly papers that will be published in a high-quality journal. At what point will the AI scientist's work be allowed to have impact, and for how long will there need to be human oversight and authors attached to the process? As perspectives on the autonomy and personhood of AI evolve, more room may be made in scholarship for such systems.[11]

Science for Science's Sake?

One unintended consequence that has been theorized regarding the AI scientist as an autonomous researcher is its potential for neutrality. This is because AI scientists lack human motivation. With AI there is no human *intelligence*, and this can be a good thing, as the work carried out will be produced without ego or ambition. In cases where AI scientists are helming the work, they will not be seeking prestige, priority, or ownership (at least for now). Any incentive to publish on the part of the AI scientist will not reflect the need for human authors to publish to secure their reputations, or to continue their employment. In removing the ego from the equation, the scholarly record might well be spared any number of low-impact publications that human scholars might be tempted to push out anyway.

With a possible new emphasis on the creation of high-quality research, the question emerges of whether human researchers might internalize a less aggressive approach to publishing. If possible changes to assessing scholarly impact play out (discussed subsequently), then incentives to produce good work in their field will surpass the current need for courting impact using current metrics (e.g., Journal Impact Factor (JIF) and h-index).[12]

Evolving Fields of Inquiry

As AI evolves, so does scholarship surrounding it. Rapid advances stemming from the accessibility of generative AI (GenAI) have led to new fields of endeavor and have also inspired work around the retrofitting of existing areas of scholarship to be able to address AI's reach. The fields of study discussed in this section are rooted in the social sciences and humanities (SSH) and are deeply interdisciplinary – to the esteemed scholarly pedigrees they already represent, AI allows the addition of new and compelling approaches to thinking about technology and its impact on users and society.

AI Ethics and the Environment

The impact of AI on the environment is of grave concern, and with interest in AI showing no sign of slowing, fears for the environment are multiplying. Another related question considers AI's use of natural resources and its ecological impact. The environmental sustainability of AI has been broached as a fundamental threat to the planet and our current way of life, and increasing alarm has arisen around this question. For example, efforts have emerged to document the carbon footprint of training AI, including machine learning (ML)[13] and deep learning (DL) models,[14] but no standards have been formally adopted.

The technology industry, along with AI, is examined by Kate Crawford in her book *Atlas of AI*, who points out the impact that creating such technologies has on the planet, from mining the materials that are used in the hardware to the use of energy in perfecting the software. The human costs are considered as well, from the labor that mines the ores to the armed conflicts that the profits fund.[15] Crawford includes a strong reminder that AI's development is not a foregone conclusion, and any choices to do so should be approached from the ethical context in which they are unambiguously and necessarily situated.

> When someone says, 'AI ethics,' we should assess the labor conditions for miners, contractors, and crowdworkers. When we hear 'optimization,' we should ask if these are tools for the inhumane treatment of immigrants. When there is applause for 'large-scale automation,' we should remember the resulting carbon footprint at a time when the planet is already under extreme stress. What would it mean to work towards justice across all these systems?[16]

Despite an "aura of immateriality" the extractive and exploitative nature of the industry is deeply problematic.[17] And the environmental risks are impossible to ignore.[18]

In the arms race to create more and better AI systems, the impact on the environment leads some AI ethicists to ask if AI is even a good thing. Over the past few decades, many thinkers have weighed in.

Beyond the concerns related to the environment are other warnings about AI. Often there have been messages of grave concern for the development of a worst-case scenario surrounding the creation and deployment of artificial general intelligence (AGI). Although AGI is a long way off, the concern is palpable and has been increasing steadily. Intellectuals and scholars warning against AI include the likes of Stephen Hawkings, a scholar with tremendous public appeal but lacking in credentials in AI.[19] Other public figures, both with and without the deep technical knowledge and expertise, have also issued warnings about the need for oversight.[20]

Human-AI Interaction

The venerable field of human-computer interaction (HCI) has been around for a long time, going beyond the interest that computer scientists have in the computers themselves to understand how these systems can best be used. Human-AI Interaction (HAI) (pronounced "Hi!") is emerging as a space where research can take place into the many aspects of using AI systems and can be equated more generally with human-robot interaction (HRI). Considerations include user experience (UX) with AI, human-centered AI (HCAI),[21] and others. Work on the part of industry is already quite robust, including through Amazon,[22] Microsoft,[23] IBM,[24] and Google.[25] Less, however, is available in the research space.[26] If HCI is the softer side of computer science, then HAI is likewise an intellectual space focusing on the results of the technology and the human users, not on the capacity to create it.

AI Literacy/Digital Literacy

As questions of how best to use AI continue to surface, humans will need to rely more than ever on skills of discernment in the process. Such skills will need to be developed and taught. Taking a page from the work that has already been carried out in information literacy and media literacy, scholars in library and information science (LIS)[27] and adjacent fields[28] as well as educators[29] are seeking to understand AI literacy as a kind of digital literacy.

AI, like the many technologies that have proceeded it, is tied to aspects including computational thinking and is perhaps unsurprisingly negatively impacted by the digital divide.[30] Tenets of social justice apply to considerations about access and use of AI, especially LLMs. When technologies exist that ultimately serve to exclude certain classes of users, the potential benefits that the technology might bring are unfortunately outweighed by unseen harms.

Critical Code Studies

In *Critical Code Studies*, Mark C. Marino explores the notion that computer programs and the way they are written are important; as such, they should be read critically. In these cases, code is read outright with its context and intent considered, and the whole is critiqued accordingly. Whereas computer scientists have traditionally been interested in the functionality of code, critical code studies is a branch of the digital humanities[31] that focuses on considerations of code that extend "beyond functionality."[32]

The field as described by Marino focuses on the code itself; as a legitimate area of study in the digital humanities, critical code studies can also be applied to systems where the code is not available. In these cases, researchers have to back out what is happening in the black box. One example of a digital humanities approach is Lai-Tze Fan's work to understand the ways that Amazon's Alexa is female-presenting.[33] Although the code is proprietary, by studying the system and the way it acts, inferences can be made. In the face of the use of AI-powered systems such as GenAI, researchers have undertaken to understand how the black boxes function and what the underlying code is like. One example is the work by Minh Hua and Rita Raley, where they analyzed two applications, *AI Dungeon* and *This Word Does Not Exist*, to assess their models.[34] None of this is dissimilar to the "jailbreaking" work done by scholars to understand the limits of how ChatGPT is encoded to prevent racist outbursts.[35]

Critical Data Studies

Another area of study that considers aspects of technology from an interdisciplinary perspective is critical data studies (CDS). CDS is strongly associated with the social and ethical implications of big data and data science. This includes identifying "the need for strong ethical investigations into data and its discontents."[36] CDS, also sometimes termed *data archaeology*,[37] likewise sees researchers *reading* in some capacity the data that is used in big data environments and critiquing it in light of social and ethical factors involved in its creation and use.

Given that AI-powered systems make extensive use of data that is both textual and non-textual, CDS has a lot to teach those who create and use AI. Indeed, the black box metaphor that AI represents can obscure some SSH concerns. By pushing the limits and in the case of CCS and CDS examining what is produced, inferences can be made into the inner workings of systems, shedding a bit of light inside the black box.

Changing Perspectives in Scholarly Communication

With the continued contributions of AI all but assured in the realm of scholarly communication, the question of how that will change the work and perceptions of human actors looms large. Three ways these changes might be felt are in 1) the perceptions of the creation of scholarship (and what constitutes creation and creativity in the era of AI), 2) the perceptions of how quality and scholarly value can be considered (including the most relevant metrics and how can AI enable their use), and 3) the adapting realities of scholarship in a world where intelligence is readily recruited from machines. In this space, AI-powered systems are another tool that addresses drudgery and allows for creativity on the part of researchers and scholars, and as such, will surely have an impact on the content that results.

Ownership, Authorship, and Collaboration

As for the extent to which changes will be felt in scholarly communication, one thing that seems increasingly probable is revised approaches to considering ownership of written content. With the way copyright is presented in the Berne Convention, works need to be creative to be copyrightable. The complex question of authorial creativity, the resulting intellectual property, and the ownership and rights of owners for that content are changing as approaches to considering creativity modify in light of advances in LLMs. Flouting publishing norms, some authors have still listed ChatGPT as an author.[38] Such perspectives reasonably lead to questions of AI "personhood" from a number of perspectives, including James Boyle's legal take in the 2024 book entitled *The Line: AI and the Future of Personhood*.[39] Assuming that in the near term AI continues to be a tool that is used by authors, and not accountable as an author in its own right, tensions surrounding the best way to consider both AI and its outputs, including who created them, how *creative* they are, and who owns them, will be key.

Further, as the use of AI and LLMs becomes increasingly normalized, notions of authorship and possibly co-authorship will continue to evolve. As AI assistants increasingly support scholarship, how aligned with non-human contributions can their work remain? Will their intervention begin to cross a line, from being the kinds of work that qualify for a CRediT (Contributor

Role Taxonomy) role, where the work could not exist without the contribution of the LLM, versus having a level of responsibility for the piece that is on par with human authors and contributors? Human actors take on research and writing roles that require specialized skills, and that are essential to the success of a project. Is it possible that adjacent but similar contributions by LLMs might someday lead the way to a broader acknowledgment of all the contributions to scholarship, including ones carried out by nonhuman actors? Humans and AI interact, and depending on the perceived friendliness of a given chatbot, LLMs sharing the load might well be perceived as more than an assistant.

Scholarly Metrics and Impact

Metrics designed to quantify the reach of research have become increasingly limited to numbers focusing on perceptions of the work and, by extension, the successfulness of the author. With scholarly LLMs able to parse out different sections of articles, including methodology and results, and with expectations of data to be published as well, new ways to consider the quality of individual articles have the potential to gain traction. For example, the report on metrics and open science from Europe indicates that research evaluation should involve an element of "[d]iversity: accounting for variation by field, and using a range of indicators to reflect and support a plurality of research and researcher career paths across the system."[40] In other words, a limited understanding of quality and impact is removed when considering fields as discrete units of analysis that stand on their own. And AI provides a compelling approach for doing just that.

An AI-powered analysis of research projects and their publications will tell enhanced stories about research impact.[41] One can easily imagine evaluating the quality and appropriateness of the research methods, the logic of studying a particular population, or the strength of the analysis and results in a particular domain. Other evaluations can assess the uniqueness of the question asked, the thoroughness of the responses, and the appropriateness of the literature cited. Rather than rotely focus on numbers of citations over time, the nature of the citer, the nature of the venue, and potentially their importance could also factor in. After all, having one's work cited exclusively by students from other disciplines in their theses is vastly different from having one's work cited (positively and meaningfully) in high-quality publications by senior scholars in one's immediate area of study.

The ability to think differently about impact means that scholars (and AI scientists) can tell a better story about their work. If metrics are really just a surrogate for impact, then AI has the potential to permit the kinds of deep, qualitative reflections on the quality of work and its perception by those in the field that tenure and promotion committees and those higher in the university structure will surely appreciate. AI represents a promising space, allowing a shift away from metrics that unjustly evaluate journals and that assess an author's impact based on the citations of their work rather than its quality. For scholars and administrators (and editors and funders) wishing to focus on specific dimensions of quality over quantity, connections, or other aspects that might artificially influence perceptions, then AI might provide an answer.[42]

External to the question of the affordances of AI is the growth of the neoliberal approach to the academy, where universities are run like businesses and where the easiest metric to gauge for a faculty member's contribution is their contribution to the creation of new knowledge, as evidenced by their publications.[43] Fundamental notions of what it is to be a researcher and the skills needed for the work have already been showing signs of being in flux, and by adding AI to the mix, that uncertainty is exacerbated.[44]

Changes to Products of Scholarship

As AI increasingly becomes part of everyday life and as scholarship adopts new approaches to its use, the impact on the scholarly record will be felt. In the process, the extent to which expectations about the time that scholarship takes may adapt, possibly with new generations of scholars using AI-powered systems being expected to publish more quickly than before. If the arms race continues in an effort to produce more research faster, and if current trajectories continue to develop as they have, such a future can certainly be imagined. And if the reward system evolves to address the writing habits of scholars who produce more quickly (indeed, as they have been), a time when only short-form, easily produced content is created can be imagined. Arguments have already been made that this time has come, but with AI's support, an acceleration of this trend seems likely.

A related point is the way that practices in the scholarly communication process will surely adapt to new styles of writing and research. Concern has already been voiced over the possibility of an "exponential surge in low-impact scientific works written using AI."[45] This surge in low-quality pieces, however, has already been felt in scholarly writing for decades but has the potential to expand further, given AI-powered tools. Under AI's influence, a related consideration is publication patterns continuing to shift away from solo-authored works to collaborations. Increasingly, there are more authors per article.[46] Increased collaboration, between human participants and AI ones, will ultimately have an impact on the shape of the scholarly record going forward.

Accelerating Change

The full extent to which AI will affect scholarship will unfold fully in time, with changes to technology and to the mentalities of scholars, their publishers, and their audiences leading the way. GenAI and especially LLMs have ushered in a period of change affecting all of society, right as AI technologies have improved across the board. As technology continues to evolve and as scholarly communication practices adapt and scholarship expands to encompass new approaches and mentalities, the field will remain in flux. The changes that will be wrought with fuller adoptions of AI will not only affect scholarly communication but also society at large. How these new approaches to creation will affect authors, publishers, and readers is really just a reflection of larger changes.

As AI continues to advance and as society adjusts its behaviors and expectations, it is only natural that scholarly communication's approach to AI will change and grow as well. At present, "[c]omputers require precision and unambiguousness and therefore have a hard time to adapt to unfolding and unintended situations."[47] How much longer will this be the case? And how best will the actors in the scholarly communication ecosystem come together to make use of the affordances during this period of rapid transition? Until the promise of AI can be more thoroughly realized, though, writing with intelligence will continue to mean human scholars using AI intelligently – as a partner in the research and writing process.

Notes

1 "ARL/CNI AI Scenarios: Strategic Context," *Association of Research Libraries* (blog), accessed August 27, 2024, https://www.arl.org/resources/arl-cni-ai-scenarios-strategic-context/.
2 Mustafa Suleyman, *The Coming Wave: Technology, Power, and the Twenty-First Century's Greatest Dilemma*, 1st ed. (New York: Crown, 2023).
3 Yujia Li et al., "Competition-Level Code Generation with AlphaCode," *Science* 378, no. 6624 (December 9, 2022): 1092–97, https://doi.org/10.1126/science.abq1158.
4 Matthew Hutson, "AI Learns to Write Computer Code in 'Stunning' Advance," *Science News*, December 8, 2022, https://www.science.org/content/article/ai-learns-write-computer-code-stunning-advance.
5 Suleyman, *The Coming Wave.*
6 For example, Tomer Simon, "The Scientist of the Scientist," *AI & Society* 39, no. 2 (April 2024): 803–4, https://doi.org/10.1007/s00146-022-01544-6.
7 Michael Polanyi, *The Tacit Dimension, Anchor Books Ed., A540* (Garden City, NY: Doubleday Anchor, 1967).
8 Simon, "The Scientist of the Scientist."
9 National Academies, "AI for Scientific Discovery – A Workshop," October 12, 2023, https://www.nationalacademies.org/event/40455_10-2023_ai-for-scientific-discovery-a-workshop.
10 *Artificial Intelligence for Scientific Discovery* (Washington, DC, 2023), https://vimeo.com/875997683.

11 James Boyle, *The Line: AI and the Future of Personhood* (The MIT Press, 2024), https://doi.org/10.7551/mitpress/15408.001.0001.

12 James Wilsdon et al., *Next-Generation Metrics: Responsible Metrics and Evaluation for Open Science* (Publications Office of the European Union, 2017), https://data.europa.eu/doi/10.2777/337729.

13 Peter Henderson et al., "Towards the Systematic Reporting of the Energy and Carbon Footprints of Machine Learning," *Journal of Machine Learning Research* 21, no. 248 (2020): 1–43.

14 Lasse F. Wolff Anthony, Benjamin Kanding, and Raghavendra Selvan, "Carbontracker: Tracking and Predicting the Carbon Footprint of Training Deep Learning Models," arXiv, July 6, 2020, http://arxiv.org/abs/2007.03051.

15 Kate Crawford, *Atlas of AI: Power, Politics, and the Planetary Costs of Artificial Intelligence* (New Haven: Yale University Press, 2022).

16 Crawford, *Atlas of AI*, 225.

17 Crawford, *Atlas of AI*, 217.

18 Aimee Van Wynsberghe, "Sustainable AI: AI for Sustainability and the Sustainability of AI," *AI and Ethics* 1, no. 3 (August 2021): 213–18, https://doi.org/10.1007/s43681-021-00043-6.

19 Rory Cellan-Jones, "Stephen Hawking Warns Artificial Intelligence Could End Mankind," *BBC News, SEC. Technology*, December 2, 2014, https://www.bbc.com/news/technology-30290540; Paul Rincon, "Stephen Hawking's Warnings: What He Predicted for the Future," March 15, 2018, https://www.bbc.com/news/science-environment–43408961.

20 For example, Max Tegmark, *Life 3.0: Being Human in the Age of Artificial Intelligence*, 1st ed. (New York: Alfred A. Knopf, 2017); Suleyman, *The Coming Wave*; Cade Metz and Gregory Schmidt, "Elon Musk and Others Call for Pause on A.I., Citing 'Profound Risks to Society,'" *The New York Times, SEC. Technology*, March 29, 2023, https://www.nytimes.com/2023/03/29/technology/ai-artificial-intelligence-musk-risks.html.

21 "What Is Human-Centered AI (HCAI)? – Updated 2024," *Interaction Design Foundation*, accessed December 14, 2024, https://www.interaction-design.org/literature/topics/human-centered-ai.

22 "What Is Conversational AI? – Alexa Skills Kit Official Site," *Amazon Alexa*, accessed December 14, 2024, https://developer.amazon.com/en-US/alexa/alexa-skills-kit/conversational-ai.html.

23 Jonathan Fingold, "Conversational User Experience in the Bot Framework SDK – Bot Service," September 13, 2022, https://learn.microsoft.com/en-us/azure/bot-service/bot-service-design-principles?view=azure-bot-service–4.0.

24 "IBM Design for AI," accessed December 14, 2024, https://www.ibm.com/design/ai/www.ibm.com/design/ai.

25 Google PAIR, "People + AI Guidebook," accessed December 14, 2024, https://pair.withgoogle.com.

26 For example, Tianyi Li et al., "Assessing Human-AI Interaction Early through Factorial Surveys: A Study on the Guidelines for Human-AI Interaction," *ACM Transactions on Computer-Human Interaction* 30, no. 5 (September 23, 2023): 69:1–69:45, https://doi.org/10.1145/3511605.

27 Ali Shiri, "Artificial Intelligence Literacy: A Proposed Faceted Taxonomy," *Digital Library Perspectives* 40, no. 4 (July 9, 2024): 681–99, https://doi.org/10.1108/DLP-04-2024-0067.

28 Ravinithesh Annapureddy, Alessandro Fornaroli, and Daniel Gatica-Perez, "Generative AI Literacy: Twelve Defining Competencies," *Digital Government: Research and Practice*, August 3, 2024, 3685680, https://doi.org/10.1145/3685680.

29 For example, Thomas K. F. Chiu et al., "What Are Artificial Intelligence Literacy and Competency? A Comprehensive Framework to Support Them," *Computers and Education Open* 6 (June 1, 2024): 100171, https://doi.org/10.1016/j.caeo.2024.100171; Davy Tsz Kit Ng et al., "Conceptualizing AI Literacy: An Exploratory Review," *Computers and Education: Artificial Intelligence* 2 (January 1, 2021): 100041, https://doi.org/10.1016/j.caeai.2021.100041; Sam Lindauer, "AI Literacy: A Framework to Understand, Evaluate, and Use Emerging Technology," *Digital Promise*, June 18, 2024, https://digitalpromise.org/2024/06/18/ai-literacy-a-framework-to-understand-evaluate-and-use-emerging-technology/.

30 Ismail Celik, "Exploring the Determinants of Artificial Intelligence (AI) Literacy: Digital Divide, Computational Thinking, Cognitive Absorption," *Telematics and Informatics* 83 (September 1, 2023): 102026, https://doi.org/10.1016/j.tele.2023.102026.

31 Rick Anderson, *Scholarly Communication, What Everyone Needs to Know* (Oxford: Oxford University Press, 2018).

32 Mark C. Marino, *Critical Code Studies* (Cambridge, MA: MIT Press, 2020), 22.

33 Lai-Tze Fan, "Reverse Engineering the Gendered Design of Amazon's Alexa: Methods in Testing Closed-Source Code in Grey and Black Box Systems," *Digital Humanities Quarterly* 17, no. 2 (2023), https://www.digitalhumanities.org/dhq/vol/17/2/000700/000700.html.

34 Minh Hua and Rita Raley, "How to Do Things with Deep Learning Code," *Digital Humanities Quarterly* 17, no. 2 (2023), https://digitalhumanities.org/dhq/vol/17/2/000684/000684.html.

35 "Using Web Science to Improve Platform Accountability" (Web Sci Conference Association for Computing Machinery (ACM), 2023), https://www.youtube.com/watch?v=esdtIWoXfWI.

36 Andrew Iliadis and Federica Russo, "Critical Data Studies: An Introduction," *Big Data & Society* 3, no. 2 (December 1, 2016): 2, https://doi.org/10.1177/2053951716674238.

37 For example, Benjamin Lee, "Compounded Mediation: A Data Archaeology of the Newspaper Navigator Dataset," *Digital Humanities Quarterly* 15, no. 4 (2021), https://www.digitalhumanities.org/dhq/vol/15/4/000578/000578.html.

38 Serhii Nazarovets and Jaime A. Teixeira da Silva, "ChatGPT as an 'Author': Bibliometric Analysis to Assess the Validity of Authorship," *Accountability in Research* 0, no. 0 (n.d.): 1–11, https://doi.org/10.1080/08989621.2024.2345713.

39 Boyle, *The Line*.

40 Wilsdon et al., "Next-Generation Metrics," 15.

41 Hong Zhou, "Approaching Artificial Intelligence and Open Research in Sync: Opportunities and Challenges," *The Scholarly Kitchen*, November 14, 2023, https://scholarlykitchen.sspnet.org/2023/11/14/approaching-artificial-intelligence-and-open-research-in-sync-opportunities-and-challenges/.

42 Brady D. Lund et al., "ChatGPT and a New Academic Reality: Artificial Intelligence-Written Research Papers and the Ethics of the Large Language Models in Scholarly Publishing," *Journal of the Association for Information Science and Technology* 74, no. 5 (2023): 570–81, https://doi.org/10.1002/asi.24750.

43 Joanna Bryson, "What Are Academics for? Can We Be Replaced by AI?," *Adventures in NI* (blog), January 10, 2016, https://joanna-bryson.blogspot.com/2016/01/what-are-academics-for-can-we-be.html.

44 Bryson, "What Are Academics for?"; Jennifer Chubb, Peter Cowling, and Darren Reed, "Speeding up to Keep up: Exploring the Use of AI in the Research Process," *AI & Society* 37, no. 4 (December 1, 2022): 1439–57, https://doi.org/10.1007/s00146-021-01259-0.

45 Riccardo Bertolo and Alessandro Antonelli, "Generative AI in Scientific Publishing: Disruptive or Destructive?," *Nature Reviews Urology* 21, no. 1 (January 2024): 1, https://doi.org/10.1038/s41585-023-00836-w.

46 For example, "Seven Days: August 3–9, 2012," *Nature* 488, no. 7410 (August 2012): 134–35, https://doi.org/10.1038/488134a; Jonathan Adams, "The Rise of Research Networks," *Nature* 490, no. 7420 (October 2012): 335–36, https://doi.org/10.1038/490335a; Yves Gingras, *Bibliometrics and Research Evaluation: Uses and Abuses* (MIT Press, 2016).

47 Jakob Svensson, "Artificial Intelligence Is an Oxymoron: The Importance of an Organic Body When Facing Unknown Situations as They Unfold in the Present Moment," *AI & Society* 38, no. 1 (February 2023): 367, https://doi.org/10.1007/s00146-021-01311-z.

Index

FSC
www.fsc.org
MIX
Papier | Fördert gute Waldnutzung
FSC® C083411

Kolibri 360 GmbH
Ferdinand-Jühlke-Straße 7
99095 Erfurt, Deutschland
produktsicherheit@kolibri360.de